Beginning Microsoft Dataverse

Exploiting Microsoft's Low-code Database for the Power Platform

Brian Hodel

Apress®

Beginning Microsoft Dataverse: Exploiting Microsoft's Low-code Database for the Power Platform

Brian Hodel
Bothell, WA, USA

ISBN-13 (pbk): 978-1-4842-9333-1
https://doi.org/10.1007/978-1-4842-9334-8

ISBN-13 (electronic): 978-1-4842-9334-8

Managing Director, Apress Media LLC: Welmoed Spahr
Acquisitions Editor: Jonathan Gennick
Development Editor: Laura Berendson
Editorial Assistant: Shaul Elson
Copy Editor: April Rondeau

Cover image by Solen Feyissa on Unsplash

Distributed to the book trade worldwide by Springer Science+Business Media New York, 1 New York Plaza, Suite 4600, New York, NY 10004-1562, USA. Phone 1-800-SPRINGER, fax (201) 348-4505, email orders-ny@ springer-sbm.com, or visit www.springeronline.com. Apress Media, LLC is a California LLC and the sole member (owner) is Springer Science+Business Media Finance Inc (SSBM Finance Inc). SSBM Finance Inc is a **Delaware** corporation.

For information on translations, please e-mail booktranslations@springernature.com; for reprint, paperback, or audio rights, please e-mail bookpermissions@springernature.com.

Apress titles may be purchased in bulk for academic, corporate, or promotional use. eBook versions and licenses are also available for most titles. For more information, reference our Print and eBook Bulk Sales web page at http://www.apress.com/bulk-sales.

Any source code or other supplementary material referenced by the author in this book is available to readers on GitHub. For more detailed information, please visit http://www.apress.com/source-code.

Printed on acid-free paper

Table of Contents

About the Author

Brian Hodel is a Microsoft Power Platform developer who is passionate about solving problems. His background in Lean Six Sigma and interest in application development converged as he began using what would eventually come to be known as the Power Platform. Since then, he has been developing enterprise solutions based on Dataverse in the Power Platform, speaking at conferences, participating on customer advisory boards with Microsoft product development teams, and leading the internal Power Champions group at his current company.

About the Technical Reviewer

Doug Holland is a software architect with over 20 years of professional experience, including 13 years at Microsoft Corporation. He is a former Microsoft MVP and Intel Black Belt Developer and holds a master's degree in software engineering from Oxford University.

Introduction

As businesses have evolved to be more nimble in response to changes in customers, economies, and workforces, they have put more pressure on technology organizations to evolve faster and be bigger than ever before. Information technology (IT) is no longer an isolated services organization that can move at a glacial pace, delivering a new monolithic system every few years that the business must learn to adapt to. Technology must be released quickly, adjusted frequently, and be maintainable by many. This book shows how to utilize Microsoft Dataverse in the Microsoft Power Platform to enable technology organizations to move and change faster than ever before. By learning how to use this low-code/no-code development platform, you will be able to deliver solutions with, not to, business teams, challenge the status quo, and step confidently into the future with a solid foothold in the next generation of platform development tools.

Where It All Started

While most platforms start with the core and expand features and capabilities as they grow, the Microsoft Power Platform was built . . . differently. It began with a need to End of Life Microsoft InfoPath, which led to the release of PowerApps, which, initially, was a basic What You See Is What You Get (WYSIWYG) tool to build forms to view and edit data. Then came the need to update SharePoint Workflows Designer, which led to Microsoft Flow, a graphically based workflow development tool. These were two independent products that were part of the Microsoft Office suite, but that just sort of existed as replacements for legacy products. However, the ease with which these tools allowed the development of things that previously had been fairly specialized opened up a new question: What if we did things completely differently?

With long lead times, high development costs, and overly complex designs, IT departments were not meeting the needs of modern businesses, which focus on making small, continuous changes. IT was holding business back. Microsoft could see more evidence of this in its Power BI product. Building reports was no longer just for developers. Business analysts, who were closer to the work and understood what the data meant, could design and build reports faster, easier, and better than IT ever could.

Microsoft had the basic building blocks: applications, workflows, and reports, but it still needed to put them together in a meaningful way. In comes Dynamics 365, and, with it, Common Data Service, soon to be called Dataverse. These tools, together, represent a tremendous amount of power with a relatively low entry threshold. This means you are no longer required to rely on a small group of highly skilled developers to solve software-related problems.

A Little Bit of History

In the past, businesses built tools and processes and ran their business the same way for years or decades. Henry Ford was a great example of this and is the reason for the slogan "Any customer can have a car painted any color that he wants, so long as it is black." The production lines for the Model-T were set up to be fast and cheap to make as much of a product as possible. What he did worked well, and others followed his methods. However, in the mid-1900s, things began to change. Companies like Toyota in Japan began looking at new ways of doing mass production that were more flexible and gave consumers more options without sacrificing quality or efficiency. Lean manufacturing showed the world how making small changes, consistently, enabled companies to be flexible and efficient.

However, this constant change presented another problem in that things were always changing. You could no longer build one tool and walk away expecting it to work for years. You needed to be able to constantly tweak that tool as products and processes changed around it. In order to do this, companies like Toyota gave more control to their front-line employees to come up with ideas and solve problems themselves. Factory floor workers would solve their own problems, with the support of leadership, working on change from the bottom up, instead of the old top-down. Front-line workers were empowered by their leadership, who gave them tools and methods to make things better.

Skip forward a few decades and you see a lot of parallels in the business systems sector. As software development has progressed from assembly language to C to Java, the layers of abstraction have gotten deeper. Developers no longer have to code everything from scratch and define every aspect of what happens to, say, a variable. As coding language has advanced over time, it has become more flexible and does more of the work for you, so you don't have to spend time doing what others have done before you.

The time-to-value is faster and the barrier to entry into the field of software development has gotten lower, which means that the tools are, once again, placed in the hands of the front-line workers. Enter the "Low-Code Revolution."

Low-code Revolution

The "Low-Code Revolution," or, more recently, "Low-Code / No-Code Revolution" as the capabilities of the platform have expanded, is a term that Microsoft has adopted to describe the application development tools in the Power Platform. Just as assembly language led to functions, which led to libraries, the evolution of application development has moved from pure code to WYSIWYG, making development tools more accessible to everyone. Microsoft began taking all those pieces and putting them together to create an amazing self-serve productivity platform where users could build apps, workflows, and reports, and store data, all in one place.

The concept behind low-code / no code is not unique to the Microsoft Power Platform. There are other vendors that have solutions that support the concept of allowing the development of applications, workflows, and databases without requiring a user to have extensive knowledge or skills. However, Microsoft has, arguably, done this better than any other vendor.

What's in This Book?

One of the key tenets of Lean manufacturing is to gemba, which means, go to where the work is done. Historically, one of the problems with developing tools and technologies with large IT organizations is that requirements must be gathered and translated through several layers of the business to get to IT before they can build their version of a solution and then hand it back to the business. Anyone who has played the telephone game knows that this never works well, if at all.

This book shows you how to utilize Dataverse, and the tools surrounding it, to build enterprise-grade solutions without needing a developer background. From general concepts around how the Power Platform fits together and functions as a platform, to the details of advanced security models and data architecture, you will learn to plan, build, deploy, and maintain solutions that in the past would have required advanced development backgrounds spanning multiple disciplines.

Intended Audience

The Power Platform consists of an array of components that enable the development of a variety of solutions by all levels of developers, from citizen to professional. This book is for Microsoft Power Platform users who want to exploit Microsoft's low-code database offering for that platform; for power users and citizen developers who are looking for tools to quickly build scalable business solutions that don't require a strong developer background; and for Dynamics 365 developers who want to better understand the backend of that system.

CHAPTER 1

Microsoft Power Platform

This chapter discusses the basic architecture of Microsoft Power Platform and some of the primary products that are available therein. While the focus of this book is on Dataverse, it is important to be aware of the other products that are available in Power Platform and how they work together. From application development in Power Apps to process automation in Power Automate, Power Platform provides the tools to build end-to-end solutions.

In addition to covering the product assortment, this chapter will discuss how to organize your solutions across environments as well as what solutions are available to manage licensing and permissions. Application Lifecycle Management (ALM) methods are also discussed to ensure development, testing, and deployment are organized, effective, and predictable so that your production solutions are stable and reliable.

Power Platform Today

Power Platform, from its inception in 2019 until now, has grown with tremendous speed. As it stands currently, there are five major components of Power Platform.

Power Apps

Power Apps is the application development component of the platform. It is primarily a What You See is What You Get (WYSIWYG) interface, but also has the capability to handle full-code development through custom components. Far from its roots as a simple form builder, Power Apps enables users to build robust applications that can handle complex business needs and be quickly developed and changed as business needs shift. Power Apps can be broken into two distinct types: Canvas and Model-Driven.

© Brian Hodel 2023
B. Hodel, *Beginning Microsoft Dataverse*, https://doi.org/10.1007/978-1-4842-9334-8_1

- **Canvas Apps**. These are typically apps that require very specific custom interfaces and layouts. Canvas apps allow developers to design completely custom layouts, colors, fonts, animations, etc. Canvas apps can be used with Dataverse, but they can also be used on any of the hundreds of other data sources that are available through the connectors. (See Figure 1-1.)

Figure 1-1. *Canvas app*

- **Model-Driven Apps**. These are typically apps that require a more standard interface—what Microsoft calls the "unified interface." There are limitations in formatting with model-driven apps, but they are faster to build as the standard interface allows for drag-and-drop modular building of forms and components. Model-driven apps are also specific to Dataverse, so they have better integration with the Dataverse features. (See Figure 1-2.)

Figure 1-2. *Model-driven app with unified interface design*

Power Automate

Power Automate, previously known as Flow (which you will still see all over the product), is the workflow engine of Power Platform. It allows the automation of tasks like record updates, notifications, approvals, and many more. It also has powerful analytical features to discover processes, analyze them, and improve them, as well as a variety of artificial intelligence (AI) capabilities. Power Automate can be broken down into three distinct types:

- **Cloud Flow**. These run entirely in the cloud and are incredibly customizable. You can choose from thousands of trigger actions and logic paths to build out process automations quickly and easily. Its graphical interface is similar to that of Microsoft Visio in nature, so even new users can pick up this tool quickly and begin building workflows.

- **Desktop Flow**. These are Microsoft's Robotic Process Automation (RPA) tool workflows, which run on either a computer or a virtual machine. Desktop flows emulate a user's actions on a computer and allow you to

3

record or program user interactions just as if a user were sitting in front of a computer, similar to how a macro works to automate repeatable actions. This is useful in situations where you need to interact with a system that doesn't have APIs, or you need to run command line scripts on a computer—stuff that cannot be done purely in the cloud.

- **Business Process Flow (BPF).** These are primarily geared stage-gating activities in a process, such as approving activities, entering dates, or updating estimates. These flows integrate with model-driven apps and show up in a visual process path within model-driven apps (see Figure 1-3). While you can design complex process decision logic in a BPF, only the active path of the referenced record is visible to users, so the interface out of the box is clean and intuitive.

Figure 1-3. *Model-driven app with BPF components visible*

- **Power Pages.** These are websites that allow users outside your tenant to access and interact with data in Dataverse tables. There are several options for authenticating users or allowing anonymous access, so they are more versatile than the other app options available in Power Platform. Power Pages is a new, more feature rich version of the previous Portals product.

Power BI

Power BI allows users to build advanced reporting and analytics with interactive visuals and self-service features for end users, such as drilling down to further investigate data points or exporting report data to Excel to do ad-hoc analysis. Newer features such as Datamarts and Microsoft Teams integration have extended the self-serve aspects of Power BI even further, keeping with the theme of the platform.

While Power BI does not have any Dataverse-dependent features, Dataverse does natively integrate with Power BI seamlessly. Pulling a Dataverse data source into Power BI also brings any table relationships, record permissions, and many other features that make using Dataverse a clear winner as a data source for Power BI.

Power Virtual Agents

Power Virtual Agents are intelligent conversational bots that allow you to build advanced chatbots that users can interact with. These bots allow you to maintain interactive support channels for users without the need to staff with personnel.

Dataverse

Dataverse is often viewed as a database, and, technically, that is correct. However, the database is only one small part of what Dataverse is. Calling Dataverse a database is like calling the ocean a bunch of water. The ocean is indeed a body of water, but it also has a great many other things that it is and supports. The ocean supports an immense variety of life both in the water and on land, is integral to the weather, and provides a method by which to move people and goods around the world. The ocean is a foundation of the ecosystem here on Earth, and, in a similar way, Dataverse acts as a support structure for Power Platform with data storage, security and compliance, application lifecycle management (ALM) enablement, and much more. Without Dataverse, Power Platform would simply be a set of tools existing in Microsoft Office. But, with Dataverse, Power Platform is a cohesive platform that enables users to solve problems faster, better, and cheaper than they could with traditional tools available in the market.

Dataverse and Power Platform

Like any good platform, there needs to be a foundation on which to build. In the case of Power Platform, that would be Dataverse.

While many of the components in Power Platform can be used without Dataverse—for example, you can build a Canvas app using SharePoint as a data source—you won't be able to experience the full set of features. Doing so is like going on a hike without preparing. You will be able to get a lot out of the experience, but you aren't going to be able to stay out long or go very far without provisions and tools. In a similar sense, you can use Power Apps and Power Automate and the other tools, but you are going to find yourself limited in your ability to scale the solutions that you are building.

This is because Dataverse is designed to support the features of the products in the platform by delegating operations to the back end to optimize the performance and capabilities of the other tools. Using SharePoint is a great starting point, but you will begin running into scalability issues because the queries aren't fully delegable to the back end, meaning the app must pull back the full set of records before it searches them. Using SQL as a data source is much more scalable, but you will be challenged when building out complex security models and efficiently traversing related records.

Essentially, Dataverse has looked at what users might be doing in an app and built out a great deal of the functionality in the back end so that it can be processed in the cloud instead of in a user's browser. This makes the apps more performant and responsive and leads to a better user experience, as well as enables developers to build more robust apps that perform more functions. No one enjoys keeping lists of bookmarks so they can find all the tools that they need, so building single apps or simulating single apps simplifies the user experience and increases productivity.

Power Platform Environments

Power Platform has environments, which are essentially places to store your stuff. An environment is where you build your apps, flows, and chatbots, as well as where you store data (in Dataverse). It also allows you to configure who can access it or its resources, what they can do, what they can see, and so forth. It is essentially a workspace for you to build and use whatever you want.

The Problem That Environments Solve

To scale solutions effectively in an organization, you will need to consider how to manage those solutions as they grow and evolve. With a single app that has a small user base, it is easy to just make changes and push them out. If something goes wrong, you simply roll back the changes and try again. However, as your solutions get larger and have a higher level of impact on an organization, you will need to come up with better ways to add features, make updates, and try new things.

Application lifecycle management (ALM) is key to balancing the continuous changes with system stability and reliability, so having the ability to test tools before they impact production users is important. Typically, a tenant admin will have an environment strategy already set up, which varies by organization, team, and purpose. It is good to have a solid understanding of what is available when starting to build in Power Platform as not all solutions are one-size-fits-all. Usually this will be a set of production and development or production, test, and development environments. I refer to these as "environment sets."

Environment Types

There are five types of environment: default, sandbox, production, and Microsoft Teams, and trial. Each of these environments has a unique set of features and limitations, so having a good understanding of these is important to effectively using Power Platform. However, here is an overview of the different types for reference:

- **Default**. In any tenant, there is one and only one default environment. This environment is the first one installed and is meant as a sort of playground for users to be able to go in and learn the tools. It also acts as the location for any Power Automate flows that are created from a SharePoint list button.

- **Sandbox**. These are meant to be used for testing, so they have some additional features, such as the ability to reset, copy, and delete, that are not available in production environments. Typically, you would have a sandbox environment of your development work and possibly another one for your test environment. You could even get fancy and create one in a different region that gets updates prior to yours to test out new features, but that is a bit much for most use cases.

- **Production**. For any solutions that you have that are in use for production purposes, you want to make sure you are using a production environment. Production environments are specifically set up to prevent you from accidentally losing your work because they require extra steps to do any major changes, like deleting or resetting. Also, you typically want to restrict development work in a production environment to avoid any production downtime. This means restricting who has elevated permissions in these environments as well as using managed solutions (more on that later).

- **Microsoft Teams**. These environments are a bit different than the others as they are specifically set up to support the building of Power Apps built from within Microsoft Teams. These environments give you access to Dataverse for Teams, which is a free, although limited, version of Dataverse. This is a great option if you want to build small-scale apps or proofs of concept (POCs) of apps on Dataverse (more on this later).

- **Trial**. Both Trial (standard) and Trial (subscription-based) are essentially playgrounds. They are meant to be used for a limited time and then deleted. Typically these are used for learning or testing concepts, and would not be used as part of an ALM model.

Each environment is isolated from the others, so you can make any changes you want in your Development and Test environments, or even delete them, without affecting your Production environment. This also applies to data stored in Dataverse and any connections to external data. When migrating a solution from your test to your production environment, it will not carry over your data or connections, so it will not impact what you have set up in production. This makes it very convenient if you have confidential data in production that your test users don't have clearance to see.

It is also worth noting that environments don't have a Dataverse database installed by default. If you want to use Solutions, which are critical to proper ALM practices, you are going to need to install the database by going to the Power Platform Admin Center at `https://admin.powerplatform.microsoft.com/environments`, selecting your environment, and selecting Add Database, as shown in Figure 1-4.

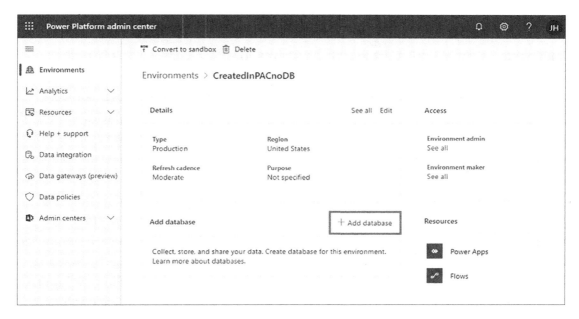

Figure 1-4. Adding a database to an environment

Application Lifecycle Management (ALM)

Application lifecycle management (ALM) is an important part of developing applications and ensuring the quality, stability, and reliability of released products. ALM consists of the following three key phases:

1. **Governance**. Requirements gathering, resource management, and administration, such as security, change tracking, audit, deployment, and rollback

2. **Development**. Identification of issues, planning, design, build, and test

3. **Maintenance**. Deployment and maintenance of apps and dependencies

Power Platform supports full ALM capabilities and has a variety of ways to implement it successfully to ensure that you are building and releasing quality products while maintaining maximum uptime. The core feature that enables effective ALM in Power Platform is a feature called solutions.

9

Solutions

Solutions are a way of storing all the artifacts, such as apps, flows, tables, etc., of a project. You can think of it as a folder of all your project documents. Having a solution keeps all your projects separate and organized, so you don't make changes that cause issues in someone else's work. They also make it easier to ensure that you have all your dependencies accounted for as you prepare to migrate between environments. You can add and remove artifacts from solutions, and even have individual artifacts existing in multiple solutions since the solutions are simply referencing the artifacts, not actually storing them.

Because solutions allow you to organize your environment assets into a folder-like structure, you don't necessarily need to have a different set of environments for each solution. You may have a team with many apps that are not related, but have a similar set of permissions, users, or datasets. If this is the case, you can simplify things by building several projects in one environment set and using solutions to organize them. Solutions can also have different Publishers, which can help to organize who owns each solution. You can choose the Default publisher, which is typically set as Default Publisher for orgxxxxx, but you can easily crate different publishers for each or groups of solutions.

Solution Types

Every environment starts with at least one solution, the default solution. This solution includes every artifact in that environment. You cannot export the default solution, so it cannot be used for ALM. Instead, you will want to create a new solution for each project to keep things organized and easy to migrate to your downstream environments, such as test and production.

Tip   The default solution is a good place to look for artifacts that you cannot find in your environment, because it contains every artifact from every other solution.

There are two different types of solutions, and each has a distinct use. When you create a new solution, it will be unmanaged:

- **Unmanaged Solutions**. Designed to be worked on and changed in your development environment. They are unrestricted, and artifacts can be created in, added to, or removed from the solution.

- **Managed Solutions**. Meant to be used in your production environments and have a variety of restrictions. You cannot create a managed solution, but rather a managed solution is created when you export your solution as a managed type from your development environment.

Although there are settings at the individual artifact level that allow or restrict specific changes in managed solutions, the primary differences are outlined in Table 1-1.

Table 1-1. *Comparison of Solution Types*

	Unmanaged	Managed
Environment Type	Development	Production / Test
Exportable	Yes	No
Editable	Yes	Limited
Layers	No	Yes
Deleting Solution Removes Artifacts from Environment	No	Yes

Deployment

There are two primary methods of deploying your solutions to downstream environments: manual and automated. While the goal of an effective ALM strategy should involve automation of deployments, I generally recommend that new developers use the manual method initially because it gives them a chance to see the individual steps as they occur and where to look for errors if they come up.

The basic method for implementing ALM is to manually export and import solutions from one environment to another using solutions. I generally recommend that new users start with this method because it is quick and easy and allows them to see the steps as they progress, one-by-one.

Manually Exporting a Solution

To manually export a solution, you will want to navigate to your source environment, select "Solutions" from the left-hand navigation pane, find your solution, select the ellipse next to it, and select "Export Solution." You will be shown a dialogue named

"Before you export," as shown in Figure 1-5. Ensure you always select "Publish all changes" before you proceed as only published changes will export with your solution file. The other option is to "Check for issues"; while this is not required, it is a good idea to run this to see if it identifies any performance or stability issues before you move on.

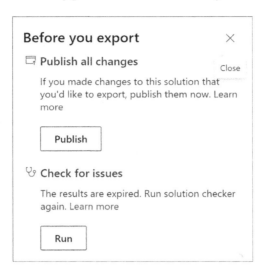

Figure 1-5. *Export solution dialogue 1*

Select "Next" to move to the next screen. On this screen you will be prompted to select either "Managed" or "Unmanaged." (See Figure 1-6.) If you are exporting to a production environment, always select "Managed." If you are exporting to a test environment, you can choose either "Managed" or "Unmanaged," depending on your preference.

Note   I typically have managed solutions in my test environments because then I can keep my production and test environments synced and will experience any import issues in test before I try to deploy to production.

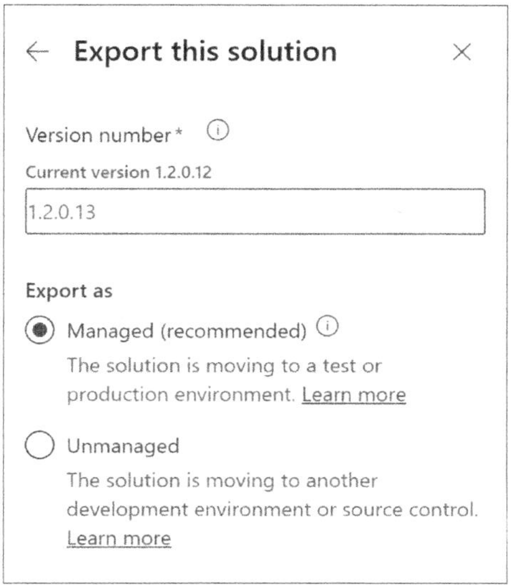

Figure 1-6. *Export solution dialogue 2*

You also have the option to set the version in this screen. However, the system will automatically increment the version number every time you export. It is set up as major. minor.build.revision, such as 2.1.2.112, as the format, so you can adjust this as necessary for your needs.

After choosing either "Managed" or "Unmanaged," and optionally adjusting the version number, select "Export," and the system will begin processing your request. After a short time, you will see a prompt appear at the top of the screen that allows you to download the solution file to your computer.

Note   I suggest exporting both a managed and an unmanaged version during each deployment and keeping them both in your version control files. This way, if your development environment becomes corrupt, you have an unmanaged version of the solution that you can use to import and start again.

Manually Importing a Solution

To import a solution, you will go to your target environment, select "Solutions" from the left-hand navigation pane, and select "Import Solution" from the top control bar. You will be prompted to select a file, at which point you will select the solution file that you downloaded in the previous section, "Manually Exporting a Solution."

If you are importing a new solution, then the dialogue will be simple, and you can just select "Import" to continue the import. However, if the solution already exists in the environment, and this is to deploy changes to the solution, you will have three Solution Action options to move forward with, as follows:

- **Upgrade**. This is the most common option and will be used in most cases. It will make any changes to the solution in the destination environment, such as updating, adding, or removing any assets to match what is in the new solution file you are importing. This process basically consists of two stages: importing the new version, then deleting the old version. They are done in sequence and automatically. If you choose this and move forward with selecting "Import," you will not need to take any further action to complete the deployment.

- **Stage for Upgrade**. This is generally used if you need to make changes to the assets or data after the new version is imported, but before the old version is deleted. One example would be that you have created a new field and removed an existing field, but you want to migrate the data from the old field to the new field. If you have selected "Stage for Upgrade," you will have both fields existing in the table until you apply the upgrade and you can migrate your data over freely. After the import operation has completed, you will find your original solution, as well as a new solution that has the same solution name as the base solution, but suffixed with _Upgrade. To complete the deployment, select the ellipse next to the base solution, the version without _Upgrade, and select "Apply Solution Upgrade" to complete the removal of the old version. This will complete your deployment.

- **Update**. This is rarely used because it replaces the older solution with the new version instead of upgrading it. This means that any assets that are not in the upgrade will not be removed from your solution, so your destination environment will no longer match what you have in your source environment. There are cases where this is a valid option, such as if you need to make updates but not, for instance, remove an existing workflow that is part of the solution. This will complete your deployment.

Note   While solution versions cannot be rolled back, environments have the capability to be restored to previous versions if necessary.

Automated Deployments

Once you are familiar with the operations and how things work when manually updating your solutions between environments, you will want to look into how to automate those deployments. Both Azure DevOps and GitHub have pre-built actions that you can utilize to build out pipelines to make your deployments easy and predictable. In addition, you can utilize other features in the tools, such as approval steps, test plans, version history, and variable updates. Utilizing these automated tools allows you to have total confidence in your ALM process and ensure the highest-quality product gets to your customers.

As you can see in Figure 1-7, the steps are basically the same as those for the manual process, but the pipelines allow you to automate the tasks and add in additional controls and steps. You can also add in approval phases between the steps if you have a team of testers that must sign off before a deployment is completed. This is often the case for controlled environments where a team of people performs user acceptance testing (UAT) to verify changes in a test environment before things are moved to production. You can see an example of this in Figure 1-8.

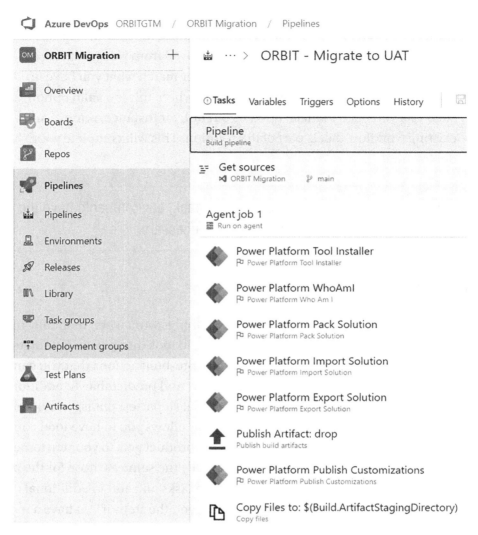

Figure 1-7. *Azure DevOps pipeline example*

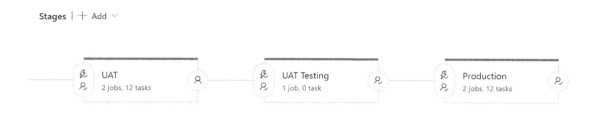

Figure 1-8. *Azure DevOps release approval stages*

For more information on how to set up automated deployments in Azure DevOps, see `https://learn.microsoft.com/en-us/power-platform/alm/devops-build-tools`.

Solution Layers

As I said before, an asset can be part of multiple solutions simultaneously. For instance, you may have a products table that is used in two different projects in the same environment. This is completely normal in app development, and in Power Platform is made visible and manageable in what are referred to as solution layers. There are two distinct types of layers in Dataverse:

- **Unmanaged Layer**. This layer contains all unmanaged customizations and assets, regardless of which solution they are a part of. Unmanaged solution assets are indistinguishable from each other, which is why it is important to use managed solutions in your destination environments.

- **Managed Layers**. All imported managed solutions, as well as system solutions, exist at this level. Every asset in the managed layers level can be tied to a layer, or layers, and can be updated or removed with said layers. Since an asset, for example a table, can exist in multiple managed layers, it is important to understand that in the runtime behavior "Last one wins" unless a merge logic is performed.

Last One Wins

Figure 1-9 illustrates an example of how solution layers would work if a property from a system table, such as Users, were to be updated. The system solution layers are always at the base because they are the default assets in an environment. If you imported Solution 1, which changed a property of a field to Max Length of 150 from its original 100, then the runtime behavior would be 150. If you were to then import Solution 2, which changed that same property to a value of 200, then the runtime behavior would change to 200.

Runtime Behavior	What the user sees	Property: Max Len = 200
Managed Layers	Solution 1 (Managed)	Property: Max Len = 200
	Solution 2 (Managed)	Property: Max Len = 150
	System Solutions	Property: Max Len = 100

Figure 1-9. *Solution layering in Dataverse*

If you were to then import Solution 1 to the environment, it would become the top layer, and, as such, would update the runtime behavior to a max length of 150, as shown in Figure 1-10.

Runtime Behavior	What the user sees	Property: Max Len = 150
Managed Layers	Solution 1 (Managed)	Property: Max Len = 150
	Solution 2 (Managed)	Property: Max Len = 200
	System Solutions	Property: Max Len = 100

Figure 1-10. *Solution layering in Dataverse after update*

The runtime behavior of an asset applies to the entire environment, not just the assets in that layer. This is why it is important to understand how changes to your solution may impact others who are working in your environment if they are using that same asset.

Unmanaged Layers

Unmanaged layers can occur in one of two ways:

- **Unmanaged Solution Import**. If unmanaged solutions are imported into an environment, they are all collapsed into the unmanaged layer. This makes updates or changes very hard to manage and impossible to roll back if needed. While you cannot import an unmanaged solution if a managed version of that solution exists, you can import an unmanaged solution that shares an asset with a managed solution.

- **Manual Changes to Assets**. While managed solutions, generally speaking, restrict changes, you can edit some properties. For example, if you were to go into your production environment and edit a Power Automate flow manually.

Doing either of these changes would result in an unmanaged layer, and the unmanaged layer always persists at the top level of the layer stack. You can see an example of this in Figure 1-11. In this example, a user went into the environment and updated the max length property to 400, which created an unmanaged layer to that asset and changed the runtime behavior to a max length of 400. Now, that unmanaged layer will persist even if the managed solutions are updated, because the unmanaged layer always stays at the top. Therefore it is risky to make unmanaged changes.

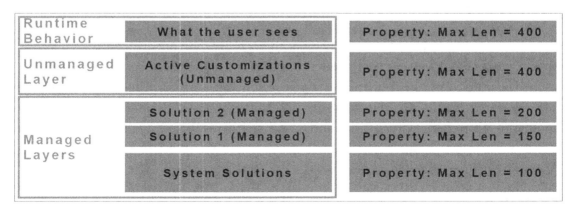

Figure 1-11. *Solution layering in Dataverse with unmanaged customizations*

Resolving Unmanaged Layers

In order to resolve unmanaged layers and return your environment back to a controlled state, you must go into each asset that has an unmanaged layer and remove that layer. You can see in Figure 1-12 that there is an unmanaged layer for the asset PDT – Change Request Updates, which is a cloud flow. To resolve this, you would select the unmanaged layer, then select "Remove Active Customizations" from the top control bar. This will remove the unmanaged layer, and you will be back to your expected behavior of managed solutions.

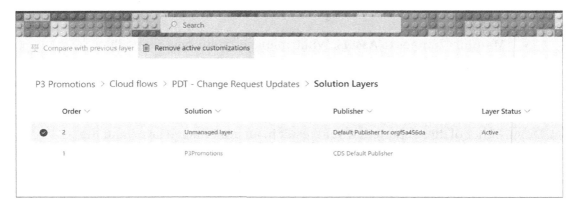

Figure 1-12. *Unmanaged layers in Dataverse*

Summary

While Power Platform has a great many tools, many more than are even discussed here, you can see how Dataverse is very much the core of the platform. And while you can use the separate components without Dataverse, you are going to struggle with building truly enterprise-grade tools. Dataverse gives you a tremendous number of features and capabilities, from model-driven apps and business process flows to scalable data storage and advanced ALM capabilities.

Now that you have a decent understanding of Power Platform and the major components that are available, we can discuss how to use those components to design and build solutions that can change the world.

CHAPTER 2

Data Layer

In the previous chapter we discussed the high level components of the Microsoft Power Platform and how they work together to enable enterprise solution development using grade low-code/no-code tools such as Power Automate and Power Apps. I this chapter, we start getting into the details of how to design and build the Data Layer of your solution. The data layer handles the table design and architecture, as well as storage and access to the data. In Dataverse, like in other tools in Power Platform, the abstraction layer removes a great deal of the complexity of building and configuring the database from the users and allows them to focus on what they need, not how it is done. Creating tables, configuring fields, and managing keys can get a bit confusing for someone who isn't familiar with SQL development, but is very intuitive in Dataverse. In short, you don't have to worry about the backend because Dataverse handles that for you. So, in this chapter, we will simply discuss the Dataverse interfaces and how to set up your data structures; we won't worry about the layer beneath Dataverse where the actual data is stored, or how it operates.

Tables

Because Dataverse is an abstraction of data storage, it is important to be aware that you may run into different terminology as you browse documentation. You can see this terminology breakdown in Table 2-1.

Table 2-1. *Dataverse Terminology*

Power Apps UI	Dataverse SDK	Dataverse Web API
Table	Entity	EntityType
Column	Attribute	Property
Row	Record	Record
Choices	OptionSet/Picklist	OptionSet
Yes/No	Boolean	Boolean

© Brian Hodel 2023
B. Hodel, *Beginning Microsoft Dataverse*, https://doi.org/10.1007/978-1-4842-9334-8_2

Tables are essentially structures that hold data. Each table is defined by a set of columns that specify the type of data that can be stored in it. As data is added, it is stored in the form of rows. The size of a table, therefore, is a combination of the number of columns and number of rows, as a table is a matrix of the two concepts.

Creating a Table

To create a table, go into your solution, select "New" and then "Table." You will see a dialogue like the one shown in Figure 2-1 to configure your table properties.

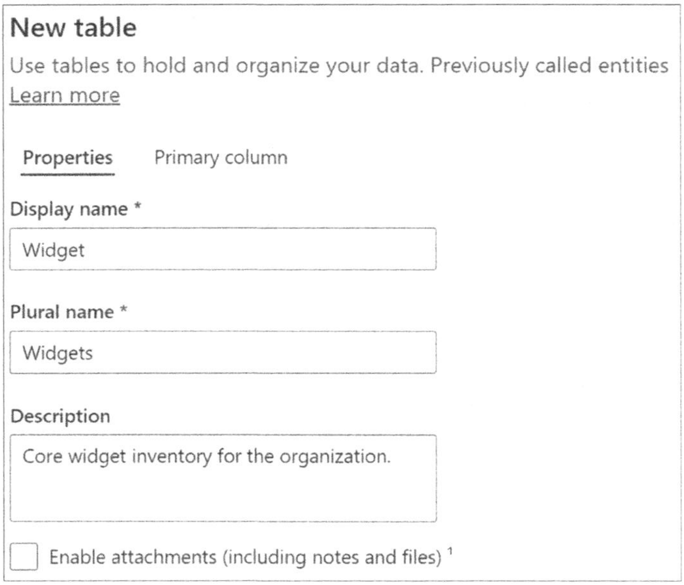

Figure 2-1. *New table basic properties*

All tables have a base set of attributes that describe them, as follows:

- **Display Name**: This is the friendly name of the table and generally refers to the content of the table, such as Account or User. It is best to name tables in singular form since there is also a plural name in Dataverse. I also find that using Pascal case naming, such as PascalCaseExample, eliminates annoying spaces when referring to tables in code.

- **Plural Name**: This is the plural of the friendly name, such as Accounts or Users. The plural name can be different than the display name, but this can get confusing when referencing tables in the future.

- **Description**: This is an open text field purely for reference purposes. It is a good idea to populate this to help document the table's purpose and content.

- **Enable Attachments**: This option creates a one-to-many relationship to the Notes table and stores the attachments in Notes records. While this does have its uses, it is a bit complex from an architecture standpoint. If you simply want to store an attachment in a record, you can add a File or Image Type column in your table and use that to store the files.

Filling out this information is enough to configure a standard table with basic options enabled. However, it is good to be familiar with the advanced table options as some options cannot be changed after the fact, such as table type or record ownership settings. Figure 2-2 shows the first section of advanced options for table creation.

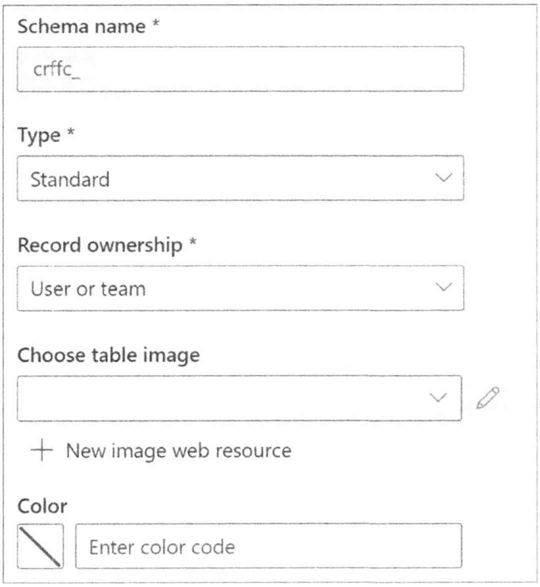

Schema name *

> crffc_

Type *

> Standard

Record ownership *

> User or team

Choose table image

>

+ New image web resource

Color

> Enter color code

Figure 2-2. *Advanced table options, section 1*

Schema name is automatically populated from the display name as you type it. However, like the plural name, it too can be changed, although it is advisable to leave this synced to the display name to avoid confusion in the future. The schema name also has a prefix portion that is set automatically depending on what is set as the publisher of your solution. Generally this will be set as Default Publisher for orgxxxxx... but can be changed if you are working on different projects or need different publishers for some reason. Refer to Chapter 2, Application Lifecycle Management (ALM) section for more details on solutions and publishers for. This prefix, however, cannot be changed after the fact, even if you change publishers. So, it is advisable to pick a publisher and stick with it so that all your solution assets share the same prefix.

Table Types

There are multiple types of tables in Dataverse and each has its own purpose. It is important to understand and plan for the correct type of table to meet the needs of your architecture. While you can use custom tables for your entire solution, you will not be able to utilize the out-of-the-box features that come with the other types, which may make your development work harder and more complex.

Standard

There are a number of standard, or out-of-the-box, tables that are included in an environment. These are tables such as Users, Accounts, and Contacts, which are created when an environment is created and are available to help standardize data structures as part of the common data model. Any custom tables that are imported into an environment as part of a managed solution also show up as a standard table.

Custom

Any table that is created from scratch in an environment is classified as custom. Custom tables still have default columns, such as Modified By, Created By, and Created On, but they are mostly configured to store data in a structure that does not conform to the structures contained in the standard tables.

Tip   Whenever possible, use the out-of-the-box tables when building out your data structures. This helps to keep your data structures consistent across the platform and allows you to use some of the other out-of-the-box features associated with those tables.

Activity

Activity tables are intended to store data that can be organized on a calendar, such as appointments and phone calls, as seen in Table 2-2. They have columns such as Start Time, End Time, and Due Date to facilitate scheduling, as well as a variety of other columns that are commonly associated with activities.

Note   Since activity tables' date/time fields are set as part of the common data model, they are pre-configured with the Time Zone Adjustment set to User Local, so the UTC Conversion Time Zone Code should be utilized to specify the time zone information for records.

Table 2-2. *Default Activity Tables*

Name	Description	Display in Activity Menus	Reference
Appointment	Scheduled event with start/end times	Yes	Appointment
Email	Emails	Yes	Email
Fax	Outcome and page count, as well as digital copy of fax, if desired	Yes	Fax
Letter	Letter delivery as well as digital copy of letter, if desired	Yes	Letter
Phone Call	Phone calls	Yes	PhoneCall
Recurring Appointment	Master appointment related to a reoccurring series of reoccurring appointments	Yes	RecurringAppointmentMaster
Task	General task	Yes	Task

Virtual

Virtual tables enable you to work with external data sources within Dataverse without the need to duplicate the data in Dataverse tables. Virtual tables give you a view of the data in your external data sources and allow you to relate data to data in other Dataverse tables and even update data in the external source without having to build any sync operations.

While these are worth mentioning in the data layer discussion, they are really more of a data integration tool and are therefore discussed more in the Integration chapter.

Record Ownership

The Record Ownership setting dictates how security can be configured for the records in your table. Record Ownership has the following possible options:

- **User or Team**: This option allows you to assign an owner to each individual record. This is useful when you want row-level security (RLS) so you can configure who can view, edit, delete, etc. at an individual-record level.

- **Organization**: This option allows you to set security settings at the table level so users can perform operations such as view, edit, delete, etc. to either all or none of the records in that table. This is generally used for things like reference tables but can have other applications as well.

Note   Record ownership cannot be changed once a table is created. If you are unsure if you will need RLS on a table, it is best to choose User or Team ownership and leave yourself the option down the road.

Color and Image are completely optional aesthetic settings that can be modified at any time.

Other Advanced Table Options

Other advanced options to consider are listed in Table 2-3. It is good to be familiar with these options when you are setting up a table so as to take advantage of the features of Dataverse. Some of these options are not available to all table types and may appear disabled.

While all of these options are useful and used often, I find that a few of them are very commonly used among most applications of Dataverse; I have highlighted them in Table 2-3.

Caution   Options with an asterisk in Table 2-3 cannot be turned off if enabled. Be sure to only turn these on if you need them.

Table 2-3. *Table Advanced Option Configuration*

Property	Description
Apply duplicate detection rules	Enables duplicate detection on records in a table
Track changes*	Optimizes performant data synchronization by tracking what data has changed since last sync
Provide custom help	Allows for custom help URLs to be entered to direct users to internal help resources
Audit changes to its data	Enables auditing of data changes in table. This option only works if the environment also has Auditing enabled.
Leverage Quick Create form if available	Allows you to create Quick Create forms to enable users to use the Create button on the navigation pane in model-driven apps to create new records. For custom activity tables, that activity type will show up in the group of activity types when users select the Create button, since activity tables don't use Quick Create forms.

(continued)

Table 2-3. (*continued*)

Property	Description
Creating a new activity*	Allows relating of activities to a table's records
Doing a mail merge	Allows table to be used in mail merges
Setting up SharePoint document management	Allows storage of documents in SharePoint instead of Dataverse. This feature relies on environment-level integration settings' being configured.
Can have connections*	Shows how records are connected to records in other tables that have connections enabled
Can have a contact email*	Allows sending of emails from an address stored in the record. If an email address field doesn't exist already, one will be created after enabling this feature.
Have an access team	Enables access to team templates for the table records
Can be linked to feedback*	Lets users write feedback or provide ratings for records. Configure a table for feedback/ratings
Appear in search results	Allows records to be displayed in app search results
Can be taken offline	Allows data to be used in apps that are used offline
Can be added to a queue*	Enables adding records to queues so users can easily access them

Configuring a Custom Table

Once you have created a new table, it is time to configure it to your needs. This section will discuss how to set up the columns and make the table useful and ready to store your data.

After creating your new table, you will be taken to the table dashboard, which is divided into the following five sections, as seen in Figure 2-3:

- **Table Properties**: This section displays the basic table metadata for your table as well as the Properties menu to change settings for the table.

- **Schema**: This section allows you to configure the properties that make up the schema and structure of the table.

- **Data Experiences**: This section allows you to configure the interfaces that users will access when interacting with the data in native Dataverse interfaces, such as model-driven apps.

- **Customizations**: This section allows you to configure additional advanced settings of the table.

- **Columns and Data**: This section allows you to view a sample of the records that are in the table. This view is customizable, so you can add/remove and move the columns that are shown to customize this view. You can also edit the data directly in this view by typing directly in the cells. The Edit button in this section will open your data in a larger window to view and update records.

Figure 2-3. *New table dashboard*

Columns

Except for virtual tables, all tables in Dataverse have a standard set of columns that facilitate reporting and permissions. Columns such as Created On and Modified On allow you to track important metadata around record transactions, while Created By and Owner allow you to assign permissions to records. However, beyond that, you are free customize the table by adding any columns that you want to create a table that works for your needs.

Adding Columns

Like many things in Power Apps, there are various ways to add a column. However, I find the easiest way is to start from the Table Properties screen and go to the Columns list, as seen in Figure 2-4. From there you can see a full list of the columns in your table, which helps you to orient yourself to what you have currently and keep track of fields as you add them, as seen in Figure 2-5.

Figure 2-4. *Columns list selection*

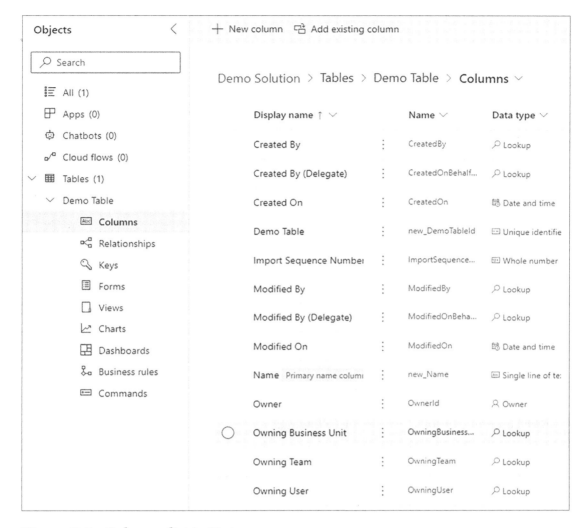

Figure 2-5. *Columns list in Dataverse*

From this screen, simply select "New Column" from the top of the screen and begin filling in the properties of your new column.

As seen in Figure 2-6, there is a section for basic column configuration settings, as well as an Advanced Options section, as with the interface for creating a new table.

Figure 2-6. *New column properties*

Basic column settings include the following:

- **Display Name**: This is the friendly name of the column, and Dataverse will automatically create a technical name based on this name. As with the table settings, the column name will have the publisher's prefix appended to the beginning of the technical name, so it is important to keep your publisher consistent while building a solution.

- **Description**: This is not a required field, but it is good practice to fill this in to help yourself and others understand what the intent of the field is.

- **Data Type**: This is the setting for the type of data that can be stored in the column. There are both basic data types, such as text, number, and date/time, as well as complex data types, such as lookup and file. These types will be discussed in more detail in the "Data Type" section.

- **Format**: This section allows you to define the format of the data that is to be stored in the column. This is different than in typical databases in that you can define the data type as text, but the format is restricted to URL or Rich Text. It is important to think about the context of your data before setting these options as they are not always editable after the column is created. This will also be discussed in more detail in the "Data Type" section.

- **Behavior**: This section allows you to select advanced behavior options other than simply storing data, such as the following:

  - **Simple**: Allows you to store data in the field via normal write operations

  - **Calculated**: Allows you to automatically calculate values based on other values in a record. For instance, you can use a calculated column if you want to create a column that has a user's full name by concatenating the user's first and last names into a single field. This can save a lot of time down the road because you don't have to maintain a separate field where you patch the user's full name in each time the record is updated. In addition, the calculations are performed at runtime, so this data will always be up-to-date as the user's first or last name changes in the system.

  - **Rollup**: Allows you to perform calculations on related records. For instance, you may want to calculate the total number of active sales orders for a specific account. This, again, is calculated a runtime, so it is always up-to-date and can save a lot of time and increase data integrity.

- **Required**: This behavior type specifies whether data is required in the field when a record is created or modified, as follows:

  - **Required**: Data must be entered into the field to save or update a record.

  - **Optional**: Data does not need to be entered in the field to save or update a record.

- **Recommended**: Data does not need to be entered into the field to save or update a record. However, an icon will be displayed in model-driven apps indicating that the field is important, and it is suggested to fill it out.

- **Searchable**: This option specifies if the field will be available to be searched in places like Advanced Find in model-driven apps. Limiting the fields that are searchable can make search results more accurate by only searching specific fields.

- **Related Table**: This option is only available if the Data Type setting is set to Lookup. This is because lookup type fields are references to other tables and need a target table to be specified. This type of field also creates a relationship to the related table, which can be used for a variety of things in apps, workflows, and calculations. You can find more about this type of field in the "Relationships" section.

The Advanced Settings section for columns is driven by the data type selected. Options can include max length and min/max values allowed. These are important to evaluate because adequate input validation helps to increase data integrity in your environment.

There are a few notable mentions in this section that I will go over here:

- **Schema Name**: This is the technical name for your field. Dataverse automatically creates this based on the display name that is entered but removes any spaces and appends the publisher prefix to it.

- **Enable Column Security**: This option allows you to restrict the users from viewing and editing data in the column via Field Security profiles. This is commonly used in places where you have sensitive dates or notes fields that are more sensitive than the overall record or table. More on this in the "Security" section.

Note   All Dataverse data is encrypted using SQL Server Transport Data Encryption, which encrypts data as it is written to disk. This is known as encryption as rest. More details on Dataverse data privacy can be found at Compliance and data privacy.

- **Enable Auditing**: This option allows you to specify whether a field is to be tracked in the audit log. You still must enable Auditing at the table level, but in the case where you only want to audit certain fields, you can use this setting to manage that.

- **Time Zone Adjustment**: This option is only visible with date/time data types, but it is important to understand the different options. Also, there are limitations to changing this setting once it is set, so be sure to plan your field before changing this. The options are as follows:

  - **Date Only**: This option will only store a date and will not store time zone information. Users from around the world will always see the same date.

  - **User Local**: This option will save data with the user's local time zone. Users around the world will see this value automatically offset for their local time zones.

  - **Time Zone Independent**: This option will store data exactly as the user has selected it in the app, without any time zone offset. Users from around the world will see the date and time exactly as it is entered.

Advanced Column Types

There are several complex data types in Dataverse that can be utilized. It is good to be familiar with these types, how they work, and what the options are, as seen here and in Figure 2-7:

- **Choice**: From a technical standpoint, this is a lookup to a reference table of values. This is the standard database functionality where you have a reference list and you store the ID of the record value from the reference list to the record field value. However, Dataverse does all of this for you and makes it very easy. There are a few options you want to be aware of for this field type, as follows:

  - **Selecting Multiple Choices Is Allowed**: This option changes the field from a single-select to a multiple-select field.

- **Sync with Global Choice**: This option specifies whether the list of choices is available to other tables or not. If you choose "Yes" it will create a global list of options that can be used across multiple fields and multiple tables. This is very helpful for keeping options synced across your environment and reducing the work of updating values as needed. Selecting "No" creates a list of options that is only available to be referenced from the field that it is created for. This can be useful if you have different values for each table. For instance, you may have five phases for one table but three phases for another table.

- **Sync This Choice With**: This option is available when you choose "Yes" on the Sync with Global Choice option and allows you to select an existing set of options if one already exists. You can also choose "New Choice," which will allow you to create a new list of options. For more on this, see the "Choices" section.

- **Formula**: This field type allows you to use PowerFX language to write formulas. While you can do calculations in other field types, the Formula column type's use of PowerFX language makes it much easier as it employs IntelliSense to suggest formulas and displays errors in real-time, which makes the experience much faster and easier.

Once you have completed setting the options, you simply click Save, and your column will be added to your table. Since you are already in the table columns list, it will be easy to tell which fields you have and which are not yet added.

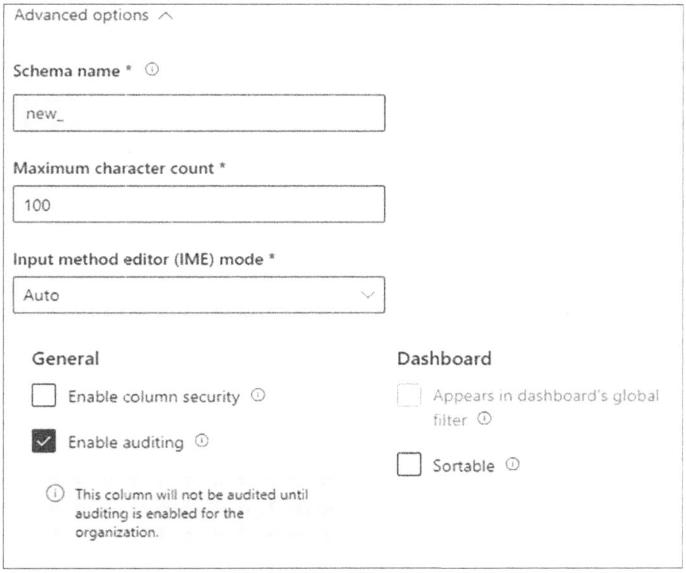

Figure 2-7. *New column advanced options*

Alternate Keys

While every record in Dataverse automatically has a unique identifier, you can create alternate keys as well. This can be useful in reporting or when integrating existing tools and applications with data.

To create a key, navigate to the table dashboard and select "Keys" to view the key list, as seen in Figure 2-8.

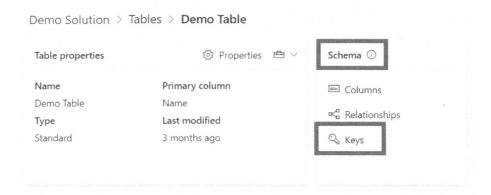

Figure 2-8. *Table dashboard keys navigation*

Select "New Key" from the toolbar, as seen in Figure 2-9.

Figure 2-9. *New key creation button*

The New Key dialogue is shown in Figure 2-10 and has the following settings:

- **Display Name**: This is the friendly name of the key. It is good to describe this key in the name so anyone accessing the data directly can see where the key values are generated from.

- **Name**: This is the technical name and is generated by Dataverse. It is generally not necessary to change this.

- **Columns**: Select the columns that you want to use to create the key. The key value will be a concatenated value generated from the fields that are selected.

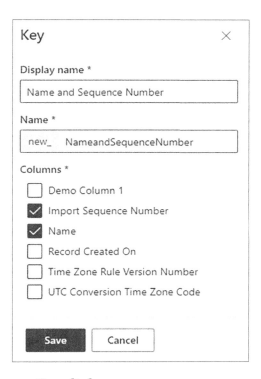

Figure 2-10. *New key creation dialogue*

Note   Keys will not be available immediately after creating them. After you click the Save button in the dialogue, a system job is initiated to create database indexes to support the key.

Relationships

Relationships in Dataverse are a valuable tool that helps to preserve data integrity, automate business processes, enforce security, and structure data in a meaningful way. Creating well-structured relationships can also increase performance and make creating apps faster and easier by informing the apps of how data across your database is interconnected.

Relationship Types

There are three types of relationship shown in the Power Apps UI. This is because relationships are created in the designer as being in the context of the table being worked on. A one-to-many relationship is simply a many-to-one relationship viewed from the other table. Both one-to-many and many-to-one are classified as "N:1" relationships, whereas the many-to-many relationship is classified as an "N:N" relationship.

One-to-Many

In a one-to-many relationship, a row in table A can be related to multiple rows in table B, but a row in table B can only be related to one row in table A. An example of this is a single account might have multiple invoices, but an invoice can have only one account.

When creating a one-to-many relationship in Dataverse, a column is created in table B that stores the ID of the record from table A, as seen in Figure 2-11.

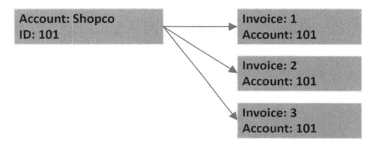

Figure 2-11. *One-to-many relationship diagram*

Many-to-One

In a many-to-one relationship, multiple rows in table A can have a relationship to a single row in table B, but a row in table B can have only one related record in table A. An example of this is multiple accounts might have the same primary contact record.

When creating a many-to-one relationship in Dataverse, a column is created in table A that stores the ID of the child row, as seen in Figure 2-12.

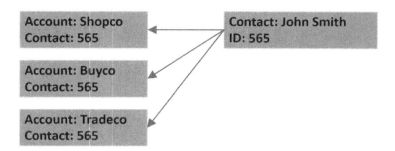

Figure 2-12. *Many-to-one relationship diagram*

From this, you can see that the many-to-one and one-to-many relationships are, in fact, the same type of relationship, only looked at from the opposite direction.

Note   In one-to-many and many-to-one relationships, the row on the "one" side is commonly referred to as the parent row and the rows on the "many" side are commonly referred to as child rows. This is because it is common to architect things like permissions to flow downstream from the primary record to the related records.

Many-to-Many

In a many-to-many relationship, a row in table A can be related to multiple rows in table B, and a row in table B can be related to multiple rows in table A. This is different from the other types of relationship because there is no restriction to have only a single record in the related table from either direction. An example of this would be multiple invoices might have multiple items on them and each item might be on multiple invoices.

A many-to-many relationship is a bit more complex because you cannot simply store a record ID in either of the rows because there are multiple IDs that need to be stored in either table's records. This means that there needs to be an intermediate table that matches the IDs from either record together, as seen in Figure 2-13.

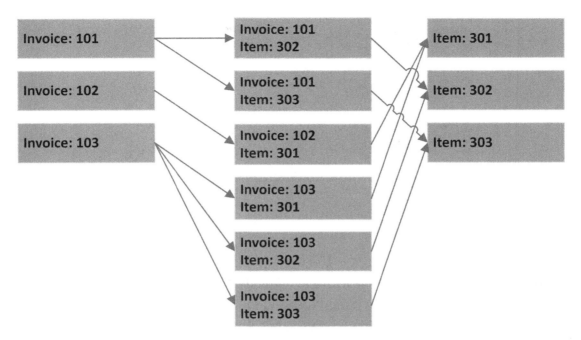

Figure 2-13. *Many-to-many relationship diagram*

Creating Relationships

To create a relationship, navigate to the table dashboard of one of the tables that you want to create the relationship to. As described in the "Relationship Types" section, you can choose either table to create the relationship from and the result is the same.

From the table dashboard, as seen in Figure 2-14, select "Relationships" to go to the relationship list for that table.

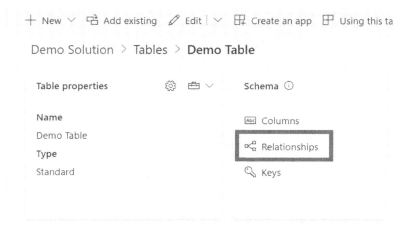

Figure 2-14. *Table properties dashboard*

Select "New Relationship" from the toolbar and select the type of relationship you want to create, as seen in Figure 2-15.

Figure 2-15. *New relationship options dialogue*

Since there are, realistically, two types of relationship, the one-to-many/many-to-one and the many-to-many, you will have different options depending on which one you select.

One-to-Many/Many-to-One Relationships

If you select one-to-many, you will see a dialogue like the one in Figure 2-16. In this example, you can see that one-to-many is selected by the title of the dialogue.

One-to-many   ×

Choose the **Related table** from which to create your relationship lookup. Learn more

Current (One)		Related (Many)
Table *		Table *
Demo Table 2	1 — *	Demo Table

Lookup column display name *

Demo Table 2

Lookup column name *

crfde_   DemoTable2

⌄ General

Relationship name *

crfde_   DemoTable2_crfde_DemoTable2_crfde_D

Lookup column description

⌄ Advanced options

Type of behavior *   ⓘ

Referential   *

Delete *

Remove Link

Done   Cancel

Figure 2-16. *One-to-many new relationship dialogue*

However, if you select a many-to-one, you will see a dialogue like the one in Figure 2-17. If you look carefully, you can see that the dialogues are simply looking at the same relationship from different sides.

Many-to-one   ✕

Choose the **Related table** to which to create your relationship lookup. Learn more

Current (Many)		Related (One)
Table *		Table *
Demo Table	* — 1	Demo Table 2 ⌄

Lookup column display name *

Demo Table 2

Lookup column name *

crfde_   DemoTable2

⌄ General

Relationship name *

crfde_   DemoTable_crfde_DemoTable2_crfde_De

Lookup column description

⌄ Advanced options

Type of behavior * ⓘ

Referential ⌄	*

Delete *

Remove Link ⌄

Done   Cancel

Figure 2-17. *Many-to-one new relationship dialogue*

The options for the one-to-many are as follows:

- **Current (One) Table**: This displays the current selected table and the type of that side of the relationship.

- **Related (Many) Table**: This is where you select the table that you want to create the relationship with. This list shows all the tables in the environment, so be careful to select the correct one.

- **Lookup Column Display Name**: This will be the name of the column that is created to store the ID of the parent record, as discussed in the "Relationship Types" section.

- **Lookup Column Name**: This is the technical name of the field and is automatically created for you like in other places in Dataverse. There is usually no need to change this.

Note   The Lookup Column properties are always listed under the table on the "many" side of the relationship on both the many-to-one and one-to-many relationships. This is because the field that holds the ID of the parent row is always on the "many" side of the relationship, as discussed in the "Relationship Types" section.

- **Relationship Name**: This is the technical name of the relationship and is auto-generated by Dataverse for you. It is typically not necessary to change this.

- **Lookup Column Description**: Since this is a new field that will be created on your table, it also has a description to help clarify what the field is for. It is good practice to fill this out.

- **Type of Behavior**: This setting dictates what will happen to the other table when action is taken.

    - **Referential**: The relationship can be used to navigate, but actions taken on one will not affect the other. For instance, if a teacher row were set to inactive, the related student rows would not be affected.

    - **Parental**: The relationship can be used to navigate, but any child records also inherit actions taken on the parent record. For instance, if a teacher row were to be deleted, then the student rows would also be deleted.

    - **Custom**: This allows you to customize the settings of the individual actions and how changes to one row affect the related rows. See Table 2.4 for the list of actions you can configure and Table 2.5 for the list of behaviors and descriptions.

Table 2-4. *Dataverse Relationship Actions*

Column	Description	Options
Assign	When the primary table row is reassigned	Cascade All, Active, User-Owned, or None
Reparent	When the lookup value of a related table in a parental relationship is changed	Cascade All, Active, User-Owned, or None
Share	When the primary table row is shared	Cascade All, Active, User-Owned, or None
Delete	When the primary table row is deleted	Cascade All, Remove Link, orRestrict
Unshare	When a primary table row is unshared	Cascade All, Active, User-Owned, or None

Table 2-5. *Dataverse Relationship Behaviors*

Behavior	Description
Cascade Active	Perform the action on all related table rows with a status of active.
Cascade All	Perform the action on all related table rows regardless of status.
Cascade None	Perform no actions on related table rows.
Remove Link	Remove the lookup value from all related rows.
Restrict	Prevent deletion of the table row when related table rows exist.
Cascade User Owned	Perform the action on all related table rows that are owned by the same user as the primary table row.

- **Delete**: This setting is visible when the behavior type is set to referential.

  - **Restrict**: Deleting a parent row is restricted while child rows still exist. This is helpful if you do not want records to end up orphaned, or existing without a parent record.

  - **Remove Link**: Deleting a parent row simply removes the link between the records.

Note   Generally speaking, each pair of tables can have multiple one-to-many or many-to-one relationships between them, but only one can be parental. If your tables already have a parental relationship established, you will not be allowed to create another relationship with actions from the Parental column, as seen in Table 2-6.

Table 2-6. *Relationship Action Classification*

Action	Parental	Not Parental
Assign	Cascade All, User-Owned, or Active	Cascade None
Delete	Cascade All	Remove Link or Restrict
Reparent	Cascade All, User-Owned, or Active	Cascade None
Share	Cascade All, User-Owned, or Active	Cascade None
Unshare	Cascade All, User-Owned, or Active	Cascade None

Many-to-Many Relationships

Because many-to-many relationships use a relationship (or intersect) table, they do not have the same settings as N:1 relationships. This makes creating the relationship much simpler.

- **Current (Many) Table**: This displays the current selected table and the type of that side of the relationship.

- **Related (Many) Table**: This is where you select the table that you want to create the relationship with. This list shows all the tables in the environment, so be careful to select the correct one.

- **Relationship Name**: This is the technical name of the relationship and is autogenerated by Dataverse for you. It is typically not necessary to change this.

- **Relationship Table Name**: This is the technical name of the relationship table; the table that joins the two selected tables together, as seen in Figure 2-18. Since this table is not visible in the interfaces and is not interacted with directly, it does not have a display name. However, knowing this table exists and where to find the name may come in handy if you run into the need to do advanced development tasks in the future.

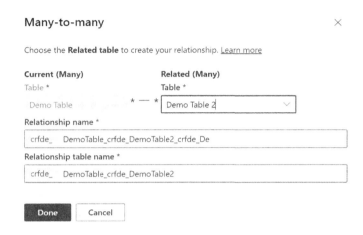

Figure 2-18. *Many-to-many relationship creation dialogue*

Summary

Now that you have learned how to build a solid data structure in Dataverse, you can move on to the next layers of your solution development with the confidence of having a reliable foundation. With effective table and relationship designs in place, you can confidently move to the business logic layer, where you can define how data is entered and maintained to ensure data integrity is maintained across your solution.

CHAPTER 3

Business Logic Layer

In the previous chapter, we discussed how to design and build your database, including building tables and relationships while designing with security in mind. In this chapter, we will discuss the Business Logic layer which consists of various tools that ensure data is entered and maintained in a predictable way. Through a series of rules, actions, and workflows, data is validated, updated, and maintained. This layer is vital to data integrity, and this section will describe various tools in Dataverse that help ensure your data is always accurate and reliable.

Business Rules

Business rules allow you to apply logic and validation to columns and their corresponding forms. While there are background processes that can accomplish some of the same behavior, business rules execute in real time. Here are some of the things you can accomplish with business rules:

- Set column values
- Clear column values
- Set column requirement levels
- Show or hide columns
- Enable or disable columns
- Validate data and show error messages
- Create business recommendations based on business intelligence

Limitations

While business rules are a robust tool, they do have some limitations to be aware of when deciding on the best tools to address your data integrity controls.

51

© Brian Hodel 2023
B. Hodel, *Beginning Microsoft Dataverse*, https://doi.org/10.1007/978-1-4842-9334-8_3

Canvas Apps Support

While most of the business rules do carry through to Canvas apps and their associated forms, it is important to note that the following actions are not available in Canvas apps:

- Show or hide columns

- Enable or disable columns

- Create business recommendations based on business intelligence.

Even though these actions are not carried through from your business rules, you can still accomplish these actions in Canvas apps through in-app logic implementation using the standard low-code/no-code methods available in Canvas apps.

Column Type Support

Again, while most column types are supported with business rules, there are a few exceptions, as follows:

- Choices (multi-select)

- File

- Language

While these fields are currently not available in business rule logic, there are ways of implementing these using other code methods. We won't cover those in this book, but there are many resources available online that walk through how to accomplish the same functionality using code.

Building Business Rules

To build a business rule, you will start out in the table dashboard for the table that you want the rules to apply to and select "Business Rules" from the Customization section, as seen in Figure 3-1.

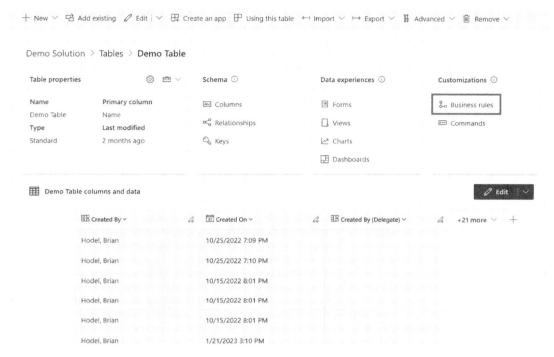

Figure 3-1. *Table dashboard selecting "Business Rules"*

Building the Rule Logic

Next, you will be brought to the business rule designer screen, as seen in Figure 3-2. In the Components flyout, you can see the options for flow and composition nodes that you can use to build your business rules out. Just like a flow chart, you will build a step-by-step logic map using conditional expressions to dictate what actions will happen under what circumstances.

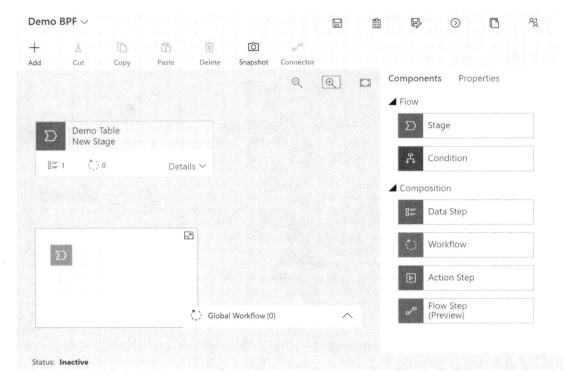

Figure 3-2. *Business rule designer screen*

To add a node to the canvas, you can select the operation you want and drag it over the canvas. As you drag the new node over the existing nodes on the canvas, you will see the placeholders light up, indicating where you can place the new node, as seen in Figure 3-3.

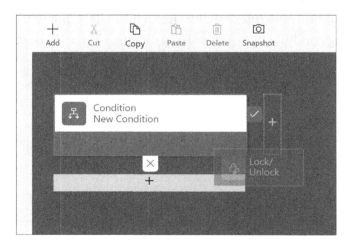

Figure 3-3. *Adding a node to the business rule canvas*

Once you place the new node, you will see that it is automatically connected to the existing node by a line, indicating the logic flow path, as seen in Figure 3-4.

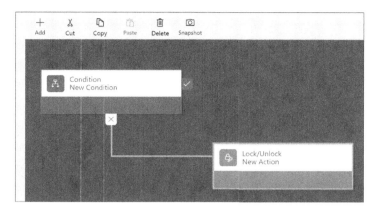

Figure 3-4. *Two nodes connect by logic path line*

By selecting any node, you will see that the Properties flyout changes to display properties for that node. An example of this is the Properties section for the condition node, as is seen in Figure 3-5.

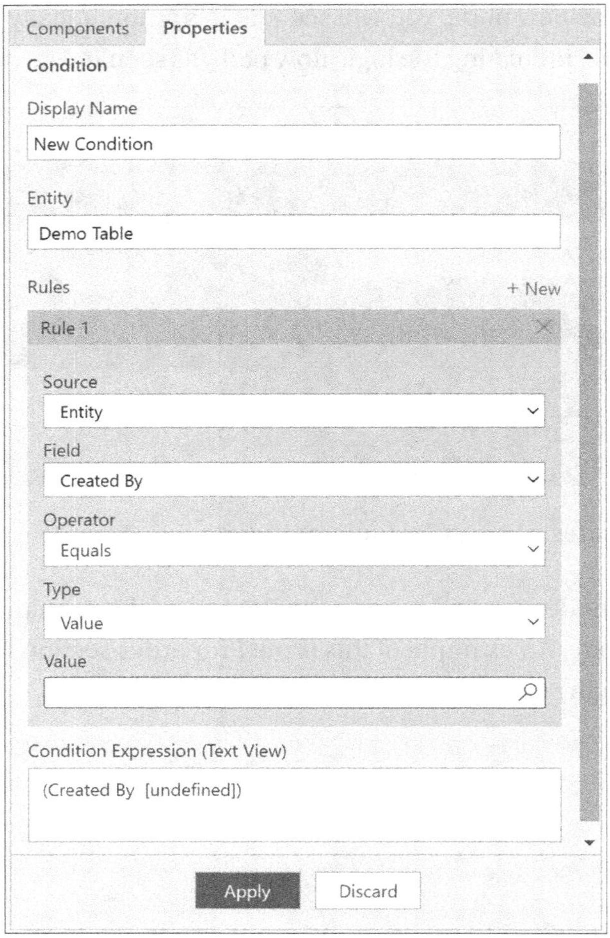

Figure 3-5. *Properties flyout for condition node*

- **Display Name**: This is just a friendly name to help you navigate your logic map. As the business rules get larger and more complicated, useful names become more important to keep your work organized.

- **Entity Name**: The Entity Name field is already filled out since you started from the table. This field is not editable.

- **Rules**: This section allows you to configure the criteria for each condition node. You must have at least one rule for each condition node, but you can add several more conditions if necessary by clicking the +New button.

- **Rule Logic**: This option shows up when you add more than one rule to the condition and dictates how the rules are related. If AND is selected, all the conditions must be met for the logic path to be taken on the TRUE side of the condition node. If the OR is select, only one of the conditions needs to be met for the logic path to be taken on the TRUE side of the condition node.

- **Condition Expression (Text View)**: This section displays the text version of the rules for the given node.

Note   It is important to always click Apply before selecting a different part of the business rules canvas. If you don't, your work will be lost for that step.

Business Rule Scope

The scope of the rule is important to consider as well. This is configured by selecting "Scope" in the upper-right tool bar. The scope options are as follows:

- **Entity**: rule applies to all model-driven app forms and server

- **All Forms**: rule applies to all model-driven app forms

- **Specific Form**: rule applies only to the specified model-driven app form

---

Note   If you are building a Canvas app, you must choose "Entity" as the scope for the logic to be applied to the app forms.

Saving and Activating

Before saving, you can validate your business rule by clicking Validate in the upper-right command bar. This will highlight any errors you may have in your logic before saving.

Note   You cannot save a business rule that is not valid, so make sure you don't get too far into building it expecting to fill in details later. It is best to work in sections, completing each section as you go.

After you have successfully saved your business rule, you must activate the rules to turn them on. The Activate button will display after your rule has been successfully saved and will appear in the upper-right toolbar, next to the Save button.

Note   You cannot edit an activated business rule. You must deactivate the business rule in order to make changes.

After activating your business rules, they will be enforced for users. However, since rule are run on demand, they will not modify any data that is already entered. However, when a form is opened where a field is required by a new business rule, the user will be unable to save any changes until that new required field is populated.

Dataverse Processes (Power Automate)

Power Automate contains a variety of tools for a variety of solutions. Business process flows (BPFs) are unique to Dataverse, but cloud flows (cloud process automation) and desktop flows (robotic process automation) are available to run separately from Dataverse, so they are a bit more flexible.

Business Process Flows

Business process flows (BPF) are like quality checks on an assembly line ensuring that a product doesn't move forward to the next step until it has been checked for all the necessary parts needed. BPFs ensure that data is entered in a consistent method and the stage cannot be advanced unless all required fields for that stage have been populated and meet the specified criteria. BPFs also help users to understand what is required as they move through the process and don't inadvertently skip a step or forget a data point.

To build a new BPF, start from inside your solution and select New ➤ Automation ➤ Process ➤ Business Process Flow, as seen in Figure 3-6.

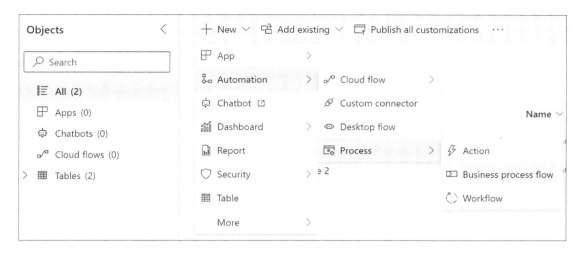

Figure 3-6. *Creating a new business process flow*

Next, you will be given a flyout to configure the new BPF with the following options, as displayed in Figure 3-7:

- **Display Name**: This is the friendly name for your BPF.

- **Name**: This is the technical name for your BPF. A name is automatically created, and there is no need to change this.

- **Table**: Select the table that you want to create your BPF for.

Figure 3-7. *Basic BPF settings*

Once you click Create, you will be taken to the BPF design canvas, where you will be able to start building your BPF, as seen in Figure 3-8.

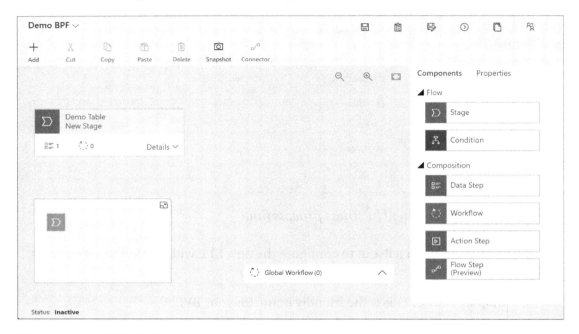

Figure 3-8. *BPF design canvas*

As you can see in Figure 3-8, there are two categories of components: flow and composition. Flow components are what you build your BPF flow out of, and composition components go inside the stage components to enforce data points or trigger events. Here is an outline of the options:

- **Stage**: These define the BPF stages that the record must go through. Each stage can have different requirements and triggered events.

- **Condition**: These decision points define the active path of the BPF by deciding which path will be assigned to the record. In a model-driven app, users will only see the stages that are on the active path and the BPF will update as the record values change.

- **Data Step**: These define which fields are required at each stage.

- **Workflow**: These target Dataverse workflows and can be set to be triggered on either stage entry or stage exit.

- **Action Step**: These allow you to trigger actions for Dataverse process automations. This is displayed as a button in the BPF stage in model-driven apps that users can select, as seen in Figure 3-9.

- **Flow Step**: These allow you to trigger a Power Automate cloud flow from a BPF step. This is displayed as a button on the BPF stage in model-driven apps that the users can select, as seen in Figure 3-10.

Figure 3-9. *Action step in model-driven app BPF step*

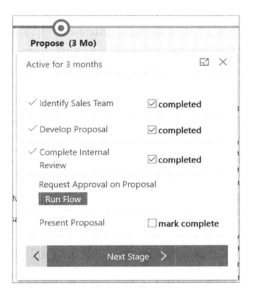

Figure 3-10. *Flow step in model-driven app BPF step*

From here, you can start building your BPF by adding components by dragging them onto the canvas area. You will notice that placeholders will light up next to the existing components where you can add new components. Simply drag the new component over the placeholder until it lights up and then release to place the component there, as seen in Figure 3-11.

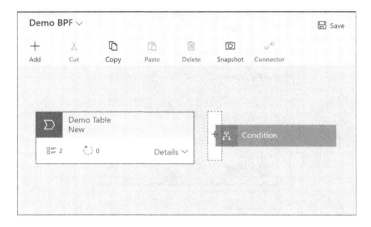

Figure 3-11. *Adding components to BPF canvas*

To insert decision points in your BPF to alter its active path for a given record, insert conditions. Configure the condition in the Properties flyout, as seen in Figure 3-12.

- **Display Name**: This is just a friendly name to help you navigate your logic map. As the business rules get larger and more complicated, useful names become more important to keep your work organized.

- **Rules**: This section allows you to configure the criteria for each condition node. You must have at least one rule for each condition, but you can add several more conditions if necessary by clicking the +New button.

- **Rule Logic**: This option shows up when you add more than one rule to the condition and dictates how the rules are related. If AND is selected, all the conditions must be met for the logic path to be taken on the TRUE side of the condition node. If the OR is selected, only one of the conditions needs to be met for the logic path to be taken on the TRUE side of the condition node.

- **Condition Expression (Text View)**: This section displays the text version of the rules for the given node.

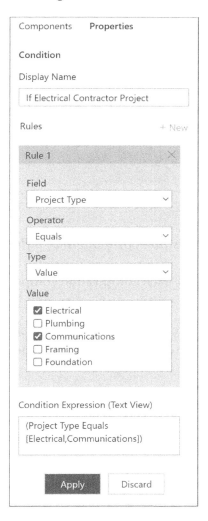

Figure 3-12. *Condition properties flyout*

Once you build out your workflow with the flow components, you can begin adding the composition components to the flow components to enforce field values and trigger actions.

To do this, select the composition component from the list and drag it to the flow component that you want to add it to. As you can see in Figure 3-13, the placeholder will highlight gray, which indicates that you can place the component there.

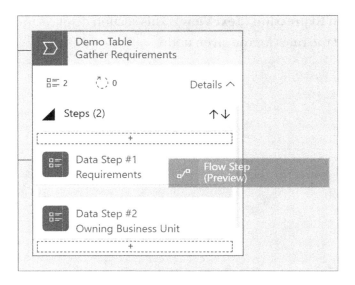

Figure 3-13. *Placing a composition component in a flow component*

As with the flow components, each composition component has configuration options to set, as follows:

- **Data Step**: Select the field you want to add and check the "Required" box if the user must enter data in the field prior to advancing the BPF stage.

- **Flow**: Select the flow you want to trigger and check the "Required" box if the user must trigger the flow prior to advancing the BPF stage.

- **Action Step**: Select the action that you want to trigger, or click the +New button to create a new action.

- **Workflow**: Select the Trigger option of either Stage Entry or Stage Exit to dictate when the workflow runs, and select the workflow from the list or click +New to create a new one.

Once you are done, you will see something like Figure 3-14. After saving your BPF, you must activate it before it becomes available for use.

Note   You cannot edit a BPF that is active. To edit a BPF, you must first deactivate it.

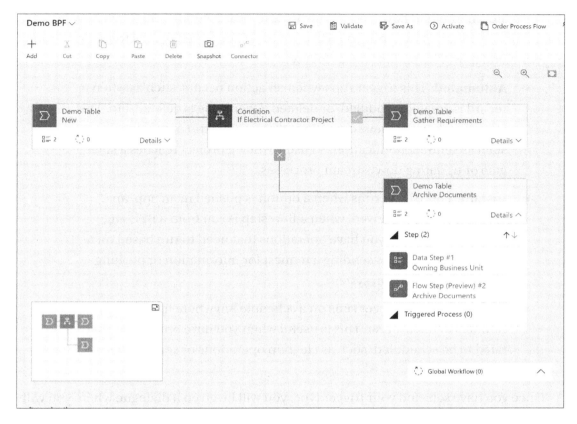

Figure 3-14. *Example of a business process flow*

Cloud Flows

Cloud flows are incredibly powerful workflows that have hundreds of integrations with different platforms and services. It is even possible to call custom APIs to perform actions that the out-of-the-box connectors cannot yet accomplish. Cloud flows are built in Power Automate and are distinguished from desktop flows in that they run entirely in the cloud and do not require access to a running desktop, either hardware or virtual. While you are able to create Dataverse workflows, they are limited in their capabilities and are slowly being replaced by Power Automate cloud flows.

As you saw in the business process flow section, you can trigger cloud flows from a BPF stage. However, you can also trigger them from a button in an app, when a record is modified, or even on a schedule to run background operations. The interface is very intuitive and easy to learn, so we will walk through building a basic cloud flow, which will give you the building blocks to create your own cloud flows.

65

To create a new cloud flow, you will navigate to your solution and select New ➤ Automation ➤ Cloud Flow. Next, you will need to decide which type of trigger you want for your cloud flow. The options are as follows:

- **Automated**: This trigger runs when an action occurs, such as when a record is created, modified, or deleted, when a file is deleted, etc. This is useful when you have operations that need to run automatically, such as sending notifications to users when a project reaches a stage gate or updating downstream processes.

- **Instant**: This trigger runs when a button is pushed in an app, an HTTP request is received, when a flow step is run from a BPF, etc. This is useful when you have operations that need to run based on a user's action, such as sending a request for information or pushing data to a downstream system.

- **Scheduled**: This trigger runs on a schedule anywhere from every few minutes to once a year. This is useful when you have operations that need to be scheduled, such as cleanup operations or sending out reports.

Once you have selected your trigger type, you will be given a dialogue where you will give the flow a name and select the trigger type from the list.

As you can see in Figure 3-15, I have given the flow a name that is descriptive of its purpose and searched the triggers to find the "When a row is added, modified, or deleted" trigger for Dataverse. This is a very common trigger in Dataverse, so I will use this one for the example. However, it is good to spend some time with the list to see what options are available.

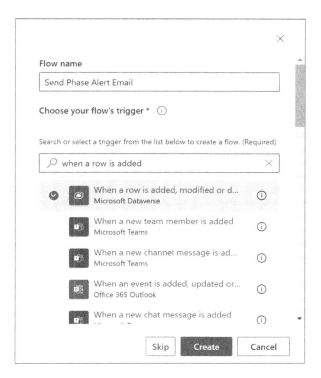

Figure 3-15. *Creating a new cloud flow*

Next, click the Create button, and Power Automate will create a new cloud flow with the trigger you selected, as seen in Figure 3-16.

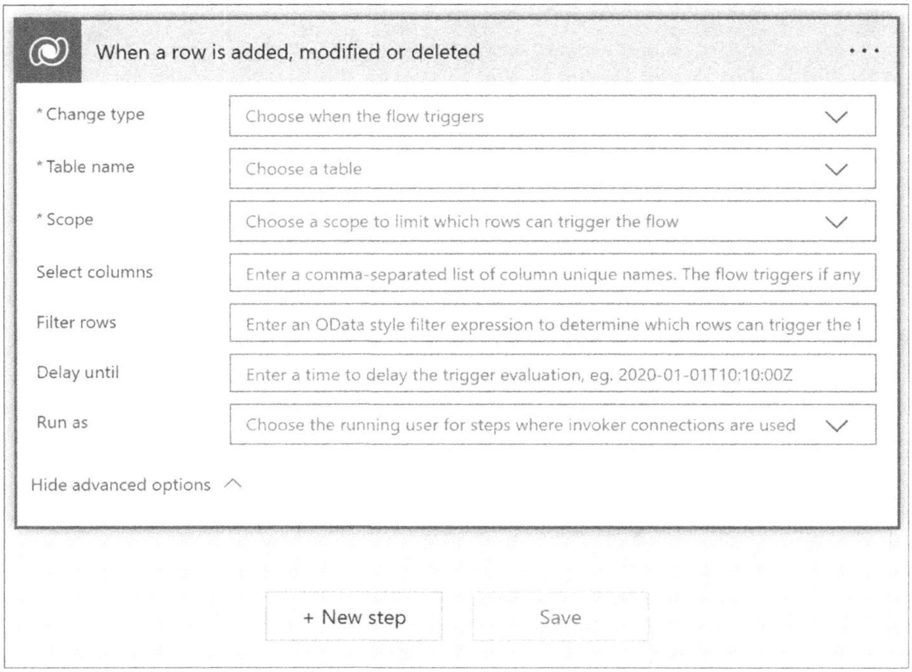

Figure 3-16. *New cloud flow with blank trigger*

Given that this is a Dataverse trigger, you must configure the options available. Note that not all the options are required, only those with a red asterisk next to them. Options are as follows:

- **Change Type**: This allows you to select the type of record change the flow will be triggered on, such as when a record is created, modified, and/or deleted.

- **Table Name**: Select the table that you want the trigger to be triggered from. A flow will only be triggered on the change to the specified table, so, if you need flows for different tables, you will need to set up multiple flows.

- **Scope**: This defines when the flow will run based on who the user is that is making the change and how they are related to your account. See Table 3-1 for the options available.

- **Select Columns**: This is where you can specify which columns you want to trigger the flow. For instance, you may only want a flow to trigger if the Phase is Complete.

- **Filter Rows**: Specify the types of records that can trigger the flow. For instance, you may only want records where the project type is Engineering to trigger the flow.

- **Delay Until**: This allows you to delay the flow run to a later date. For instance, you may want to only run flows on the weekend.

- **Run As**: This allows you to specify whose account the flow runs as. You can select Flow Owner, Modifying User, or Row Owner. This can be helpful when you need to track who is making the changes to downstream records or if the flow owner doesn't have access to certain records.

Table 3-1. *Record Scope for Cloud Flows*

Scope	Trigger Timing
Business Unit	When an action is taken on a row owned by the same business unit as the users
Organization	When an action is taken on any row, regardless of ownership
Parent: Child business unit	When an action is taken on a row owned by the same business unit as the user or a child business unit of the user's business unit
User	When an action is taken on a row owned by the user

Once you have your trigger configured, you need to set up the rest of your flow. To do this, simply click the +New Step button below the initial step, and you will be given a dialogue where you can select the next step in your flow.

The Choose an Operation dialogue will be displayed with a list of options, as seen in Figure 3-17.

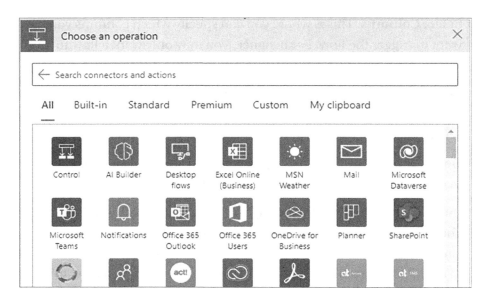

Figure 3-17. *Choose an Operation dialogue in Power Automate*

There are multiple categories of connectors and actions in this dialogue, and it is good to spend some time exploring them to get an understanding of what is available to use here. Here is an outline of the categories:

- **All**: This simply lists all the available operations.

- **Built-In**: This section has operations that involve logic, data manipulation, or interacting with other flows or apps directly.

- **Standard**: This section lists operations that use standard connectors that do not require a Premium license.

- **Premium**: This section lists operations that use premium connectors and require a Premium license to run.

- **Custom**: This section lists custom connectors that have been created in your environment. These are generally used in place of API calls and can be very powerful for performing operations that are not yet built in the connectors available in the platform.

- **My Clipboard**: This section is a clipboard where you can find items that you have copied from elsewhere in your flow or from other flows. Copy/Paste functionality can save a lot of time when building large flows or consolidating flows.

Note   Flow licensing requirements depend on who is triggering the flow run. For instance, if you have a flow with a Premium connector operation that is triggered from a button push in an app, then the user clicking the button must be licensed for premium connectors. However, if you have a flow that is triggered on record change, and a user changes a record, then the user does not have to have a Premium license, only the creator of the flow requires a license.

For this example, I am going to choose a logic operation, so I will choose Control from the list of operations in the Built-In section, as seen in Figure 3-18.

Figure 3-18. *Control operation under Built-In operations category*

After clicking the Control option, you will be given a list of actions to choose from. This behavior is consistent with all operations selections and allows you to select the specific action that you want to call, as seen in Figure 3-19.

Figure 3-19. *Control operation action list*

For this example, I will choose Condition, as that is a very commonly used option.

Note   Hovering over the "I" icon on the action will give you more details about the action and what it does.

As you can see in Figure 3-20, selecting the condition action adds a set of steps under the trigger action created earlier. This is how you will work through building your workflow, adding actions and building out your workflow just as you would do in a process-mapping program like Visio.

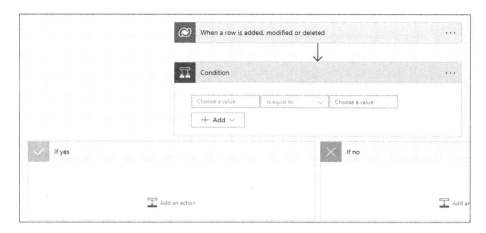

Figure 3-20. *New condition action added after the trigger action*

To configure your logic in the condition action, you will start by clicking in the left-side field of the Condition control. Once you click in the field, the Dynamic Content dialogue will appear, listing all the options for data fields that you can choose from. Environmental Variables will always show up first, followed by outputs from previous steps. You can see in Figure 3-21 the section in the Dynamic Content dialogue called "When a row is added, modified, or deleted," followed by a list of fields. That section title comes from the preceding step, which, in this case, is your trigger that is named the same. The field options shown below that are the outputs of that action and will return the values of that field when a flow is run.

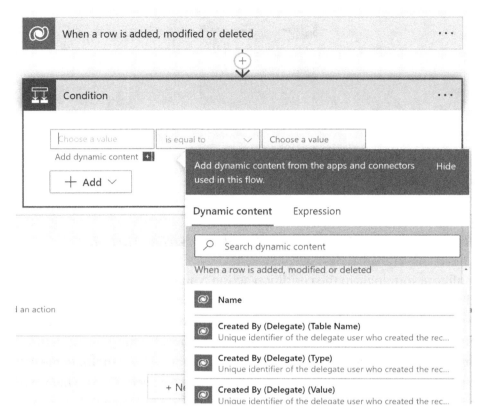

Figure 3-21. *Dynamic Content dialogue showing available fields to choose*

In this case, I will choose "Project Type," select "is equal to" in the condition field, and enter 100000000 in the right-side field. This will check to see if the project type is 100000000 and run either the "If Yes" side or the "If No" side of the logic, depending on what the logic check evaluates to.

Note   The values returned from Dataverse connectors are the values of the field. Since Project Type is a Choice field, it uses Choices as options and stores the ID of that choice in the field, not the label of the choice. So, it is good to go back to review your field options and the values when writing logic. You can see an example of the Choices table in Figure 3-22 from the field settings in the demo table created previously.

Figure 3-22. *Options labels and values in the table field settings for project type*

To complete the condition section of your flow, select the "Add an Action" button on the "If Yes" side and add any actions you want to be completed when the condition is evaluated to TRUE, and do the same for the opposite side. Repeat this process until your flow is complete. Click Save once complete and return to the flow dashboard to turn the flow on by clicking "Turn On" in the top control bar.

Note   To test your flows, you can go into the edit mode of the flow and select "Test" from the upper control bar. If your flow has run before, you can select "Automatically" and select a previous run to re-run for testing, as seen in Figure 3-23. This can help you to troubleshoot changes as you work through issues or changes to your flow.

Figure 3-23. *Testing a flow by selecting a previous run*

Desktop Flows

Desktop flows are different from cloud flows in that they involve robotic process automation. The process for creating these flows is a bit more elaborate as you need to have either a computer or a virtual machine to run these operations on. Either way, the point of the desktop flow is to log in to the specified desktop and emulate the actions of a user. This is very useful for integrating legacy applications that don't have APIs and require a user to log in to a browser to enter or retrieve information. You can also run Windows commands and operations since it is logging in to a machine to perform the operations.

While the scope of this book does not cover how to build these flows, it is worth mentioning that the tool is available and very powerful if you have a need for it.

Summary

Now, you can build out the basic components of the business logic layer in Dataverse. With these skills, you can help to ensure that your processes are followed, your data is accurate, and your tools are predictable. The next step is to create the security requirements to ensure that data is available only to those who are intended to see it.

CHAPTER 4

Security Layer

In the previous chapter, we discussed the Business Logic Layer and how business rules and processes can be used to ensure data integrity and consistency. In this chapter, we will look at the Security Layer, which creates a barrier between the user and the data. This can be in the form of restricting visibility, performing updates, deleting data, or appending records to each other. Data can be restricted at the app, field, record, and table levels, and more. There are many tools to help accomplish these goals, and those tools are often used in conjunction with each other to accomplish complex security implementations.

When it comes to Dataverse, the layers work together seamlessly and quickly. Every call to data is passed through a series of security layers to return the appropriate data to the user as well as to grant the user only the allowed operational capabilities.

Security Roles

Security roles allow you to define the permissions that are granted to a user either directly or indirectly through teams. Once you have a security role built, you can assign that role to a user or team, and where it is assigned will impact how it affects the user and in what context the role is active.

Creating Security Roles

To begin building security roles, go into your solution and select New ➤ Security ➤ Security Role, as seen in Figure 4-1.

© Brian Hodel 2023
B. Hodel, *Beginning Microsoft Dataverse*, https://doi.org/10.1007/978-1-4842-9334-8_4

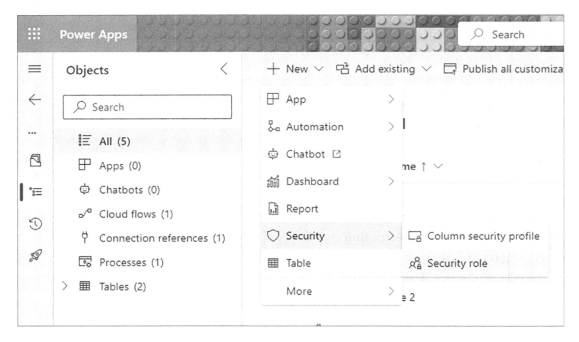

Figure 4-1. *Creating security roles*

This will open a new window that will allow you to start configuring your new security role. The primary items to fill out are as follows:

- **Role Name**: Be descriptive here as to what the role is meant for as you may end up with several different security roles and you don't want to accidentally assign a user the incorrect permissions because of confusing names.

- **Business Unit**: Specify the business unit that you want the role to apply to. By default, the top-level business unit is selected, but you can assign the role to only specific business units if you want to be more granular, such as for a matrix security structure.

- **Member's Privilege Inheritance**: Select the type of permissions inheritance for this role. There are two options:

  - **Team Privileges Only**: This security role applies to records owned/created by the user's team(s). You can use this type of role to only allow users to create team(s)-owned records but not records owned by themselves. This can be useful if users move around a lot.

- **Direct User (Basic) Access Level and Team Privileges**: This role type applies the permissions to records owned/created by the user and the user's team(s). You can grant this security role to a user and/or a team and the user will have permissions to both records that they own as well as records that their team(s) own.

Once you have the basics configured for the security role, you will move into the details of what that security role enables the user to see and/or do. There are a lot of capabilities in the security role configuration that control everything from what a user can do in an environment to what they can see in the data. For now, we will just talk about the basics of managing data security through table permissions.

Across the top of the Security Role settings screen, you will see a series of tabs. The tabs organize the types of features/tables by what they are related to, such as Sales, Service, Custom Entities (tables), etc. If you select Core Records, you will see a list of the default tables in the environment, as seen in Figure 4-2.

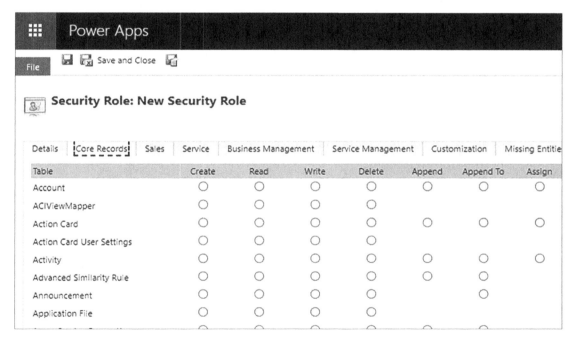

Figure 4-2. *Security Role table settings*

The general layout is a matrix of tables and their permissions. At the intersection of each permission level (top) and table name (left), there is a circle that defines the scope of that permission.

Note   Not all permission types and scopes are available for all tables. For instance, an organization-owned table does not have Share or Assign permissions available because records cannot be shared or assigned individually as the records in those tables are always owned by the organization.

Permissions scopes can be applied by simply selecting the circle where you want to apply the permission. Selecting the circle changes the scope and is indicated by a circle that progressively fills in. The scope options are outlined in the key at the bottom of the screen and operate as follows:

- **None Selected**: No permissions are granted.

- **User**: This permission level applies only to records owned by the user.

- **Business Unit**: This permissions level applies to all records owned by teams or users assigned to the user's business unit.

- **Parent:Child Business Units**: This permission applies to all records owned by teams or users assigned to the user's business unit, as well as any child business units of that business unit.

- **Organization**: This permission applies to records owned by anyone or any team within the organization and essentially bypasses the permissions hierarchy.

Applying Security Roles

Once security roles are created, they can be applied to either users or teams. Applying a security role to a user or a team applies the permission of that security role to the user or the users in the team. Since security roles enable access, not restrict access, applying multiple security roles will grant whatever the highest level of access is for each item to that user or team.

To assign a security role, go to the Power Apps Admin Center and select either Teams or Users from the environment settings, as seen in Figure 4-3.

Figure 4-3. *Selecting Teams or Users from environment settings*

In either case, once you open the Teams or Users list, you will select the record to which you wish to apply the security role, select the ellipsis next to the record, and select Manage Security Roles, as seen in Figure 4-4.

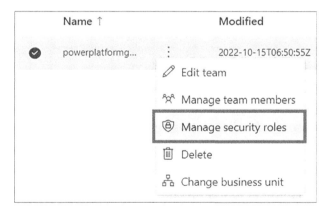

Figure 4-4. *Manage security roles*

You will be shown a dialogue listing all of the security roles available, as seen in Figure 4-5. Simply select the security role or roles and click Save, and the security roles will be applied.

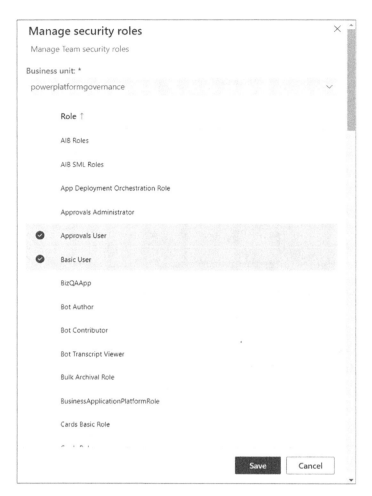

Figure 4-5. *Security role selection dialogue*

Note   Security roles applied to teams can sometimes take a while to propagate to the user. If security roles need to be applied and used immediately, such as for testing, it is best to have the user log out of and back in to their O365 profile to ensure that the roles update.

Teams

Applying security roles directly to a user's account is effective for applying permissions, but can be very difficult to manage at scale. Teams are a great way to manage permissions of groups of users quickly and easily. It also allows for easier viewing of permissions of groups of users instead of individually because you can quickly go into a team and view who is a member, or even create reports of those team's members.

Note   Administrator security roles cannot be applied to teams and must be applied to a user's record directly.

Team Types

While all team types are essentially groups of users, there are different team types for different use cases. Understanding the different team types will help you design the most stable and maintainable security design possible for your needs.

Owner Teams

Owner teams allow more flexibility in managing records as they are not tied to a user and that user's defined business unit. Instead, records can be assigned directly to an owner team. As with users, every owner team has one and only one business unit that it is associated with. In fact, by default, every business unit has an associated owner team that you can utilize for assigning records. However, you are free to create additional owner teams, as needed, to expand that model.

One of the common use cases for owner teams is to apply permissions to groups of users in bulk. Since you can apply security roles to a team directly, you can quickly and easily apply and update permissions of a group of users. You can also quickly audit and update user permissions by reviewing who is a member of which team.

User-Created Access

User-created access teams are similar to owner teams in that they are created individually, and users are added to them. However, user-created access teams do not own records. Instead, records are shared with these teams as you would share records

83

with a user. This allows a lot of flexibility in your design because they are very flexible and can be created/removed as needed without affecting the overall architecture of the system.

Auto-Created Access (System-Managed)

Auto-created access teams allow you to set up row-level security for times when a record does not have a standard permissions structure. Auto-created access teams are essentially a set of teams that are set up for each record in a specified table, and those teams are based on a team template. For instance, you may have a Read-Only team template and a Read/Write team template for a given table. Every time a new record is created, it has the potential to create one or both access teams for that record based on the access team templates established for that table.

While an access team has the potential to be created, it is not actually created until a user is assigned to that team. This reduces the number of unused teams that are created. However, as soon as a user is added to an access team for a given record, if the team does not yet exist, the team will be created and the user assigned, thereby granting that user the rights afforded to them in the definition of the team template that was specified. Figure 4-6 illustrates the structure of having two access teams, one with read-only and the other with read/write permissions, enabled for an activity table.

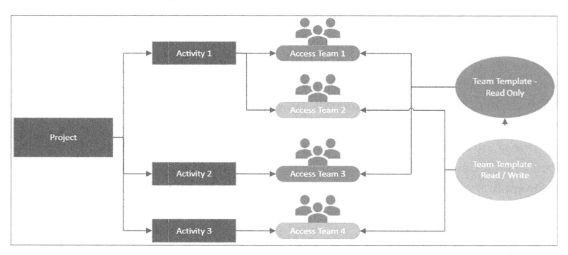

Figure 4-6. *Access team structure diagram*

In this example, you can see that Activity 1 had one of each access team type, but Activity 2 had only the read-only access team type, and Activity 3 has only the read/write access team type. Also, you can see that every access team has members associated with it. If you were to remove all the members from Access Team 2, then Access Team 2 would be removed because access teams are on-demand teams. If you were to add members to a read-only access team for Activity 3, then a new access team would be created, and the members would be associated with it. This whole process is automated for you by the system.

Group Teams (Azure AD Security and M365)

Group teams are synced from Azure AD Security groups or M365 groups into Dataverse. This allows you to utilize an existing team structure that you have for your organization instead of having to recreate it within Dataverse. This can save a lot of time and hassle if the existing model already meets your security structure needs. Table 4-1 illustrates this.

Table 4-1. *Team Types and Properties*

Team	Usage Considerations	Can Use Team Template	Can Own Records	Number of Rows Owned or Accessed	Can Have Security Role Assigned
Owner	Records need to be owned by a team, or the number of teams is variable.	No	Yes	Can own multiple records	Yes
User-Created Access	Records must be shared with a team, number of teams is variable, and access rights are not consistent across all team members.	No	No	Can access multiple records	No. Provides access rights on the record
Auto-Created Access (system-managed)	Records have unique sets of users, access rights are not consistent across all team members, and dynamic team creation is required.	Yes	No	Can access only one record	No. Provides access rights on the record
Group Teams (Azure AD Security and M365)	Records must be owned by a team and users are managed in AAD security or Office teams.	No	Yes	Can own multiple records	Yes

Creating Teams

The process for creating teams in Dataverse will vary depending on the type of team that is being created.

Owner Team Setup

To set up your owner team template, you will go to the environment settings by selecting the settings gear in the upper-right corner and then selecting "Admin center," as shown in Figure 4-7.

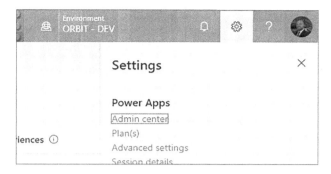

Figure 4-7. *Accessing the Power Platform Admin Center*

Next, select Environments from the left-hand navigation bar, find your environment, and select "Settings" from the menu, as seen in Figure 4-8.

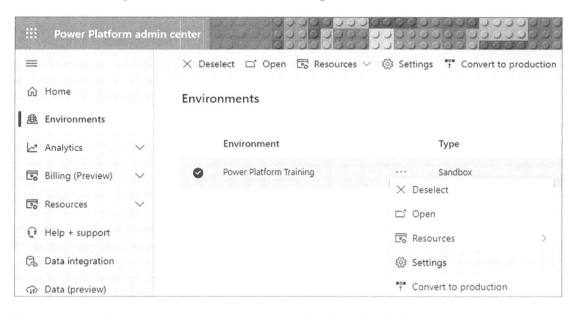

Figure 4-8. *Accessing environment settings in the Admin Center*

Search for "Teams" or select "Teams" under the Users + Permissions section, as seen in Figure 4-9.

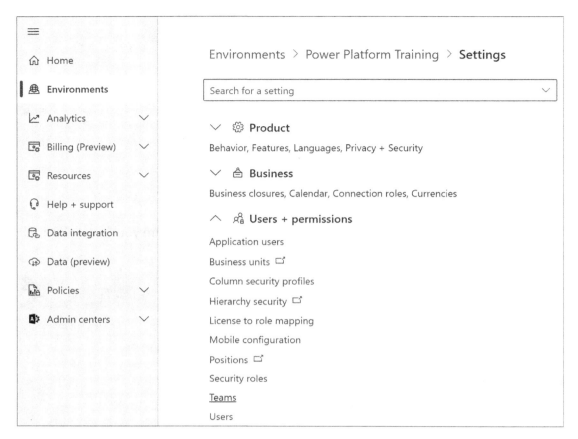

Figure 4-9. *Selecting "Teams" in environment Admin Center*

Once the Teams window opens up, select "Create Team" from the top control bar and a dialogue will open to begin the process of creating your team, as seen in Figure 4-10.

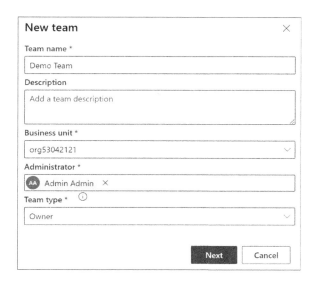

Figure 4-10. *New team settings dialogue*

You will be prompted for the following attributes to create your team:

- **Team Name**: Display name for your team

- **Description**: Describe the purpose, scope, etc. of the team.

- **Business Unit**: Specifies the business unit of the team and, in turn, the records that get assigned to the team. This becomes important when you have a hierarchy of business units to organize your record structures and permissions.

- **Administrator**: Account that is identified as the administrator of the team.

- **Team Type**: In this case you will select "Owner," but this dropdown is also used for Access, AAD Security Groups, and AAD Office Groups.

Next, you will be prompted to begin adding users to the team, as seen in Figure 4-11. You can continue to add/remove members after your team is created as well.

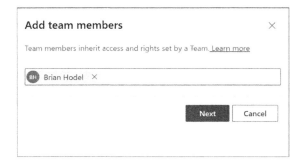

Figure 4-11. *Add Team Members dialogue*

Next, you will select the security roles that will be applied to the team, as seen in Figure 4-12. You must select at least one security role, but can select as many as you want, except for special roles, such as System Administrator.

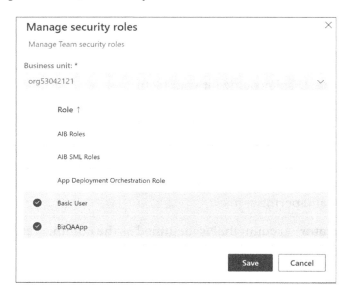

Figure 4-12. *Adding security roles to new owner team*

Once you are done, click Save, and your team will be provisioned.

User-Created Access Team Setup

Creating user-created access teams is like creating owner teams except for the selection of "Access Team" for the Team Type field in the New Team settings dialogue seen in Figure 4-13.

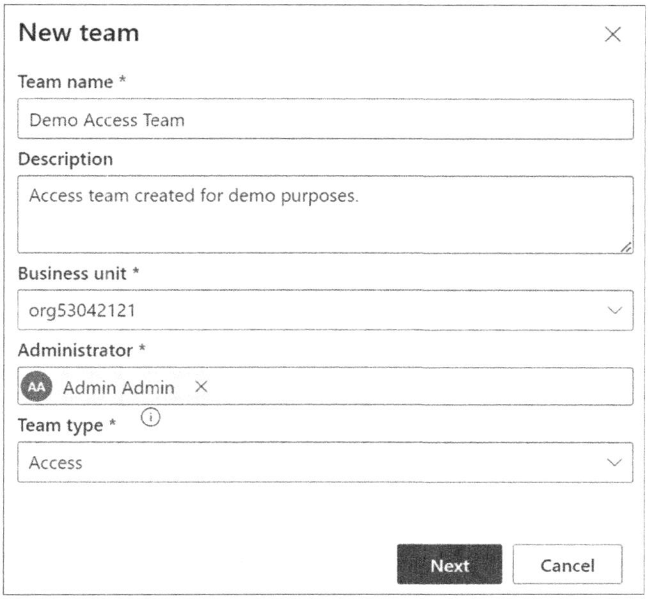

New team   ✕

Team name *

| Demo Access Team |

Description

| Access team created for demo purposes. |

Business unit *

| org53042121   ⌄ |

Administrator *

| 🅐🅐 Admin Admin   ✕ |

Team type *   ⓘ

| Access   ⌄ |

[Next]   [Cancel]

Figure 4-13. Access Team creation form

Another differentiation between owner and access teams is that access teams do not have security roles applied to them, so you will skip that step when setting up your team.

Group Team Setup

Creating group teams is like setting up owner teams, but you will select either "AAD Office Group" or "AAD Security Group" in the Team Type field in the New Team form, as seen in Figure 4-14.

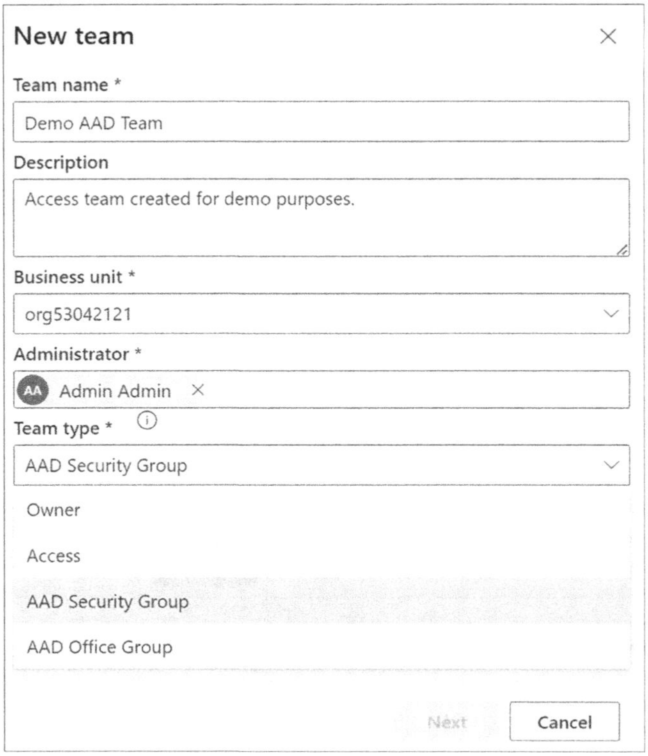

Figure 4-14. *Group Team creation form*

Once you select the team type of AAD Security Group or AAD Office Group, depending on your group type, you will be shown two additional fields: Group Name and Membership Type.

- **Group Name**: The name of the group from AAD. You can select your group by typing the name of your group in the Group Name field; a list of search suggestions will show up for you to select the correct one.

- **Membership Type**: Essentially a filter of the users that are part of the group specified in the Group Name field. Figure 4-15 shows the options for this field, which are Members and Guests, Members, Owners, or Guests. This is essentially a filter of what types of users from the specified group are added to your team in Dataverse. Members and Guests will include all users that are part of the specified group.

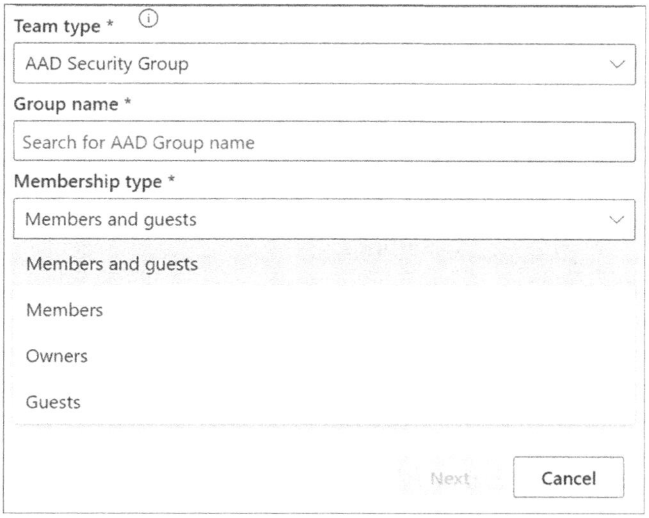

Figure 4-15. *AAD Group Type setup options*

Auto-Created Access Team Setup

Auto-created access teams are created automatically, as needed, but the templates need to be set up and assigned to the table that the teams will be associated with. To enable auto-created access teams for a table, you must first enable that setting at the table level either while creating a table or by editing the table setting and selecting the "Have an access team," as shown in Figure 4-16.

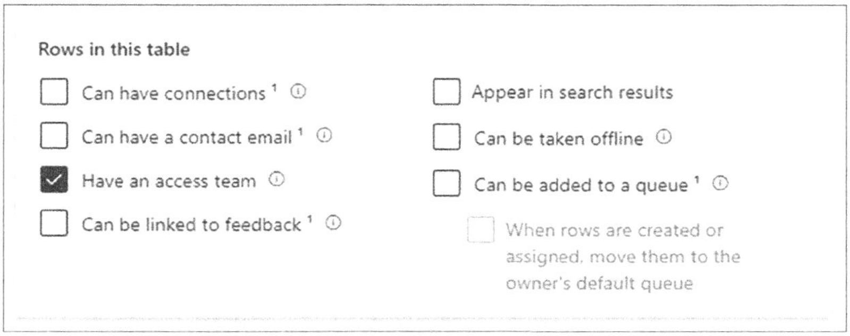

Figure 4-16. *Enabling access teams for a table*

To set up your access team template, you will go to the environment settings by selecting the settings gear in the upper-right corner and then "Admin center," as shown in Figure 4-17.

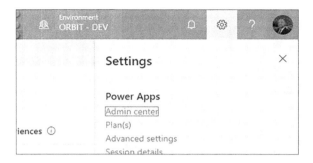

Figure 4-17. *Accessing the Power Platform Admin Center*

Next, select "Environments" from the left-hand navigation bar, find your environment, and select "Settings," as seen in Figure 4-18.

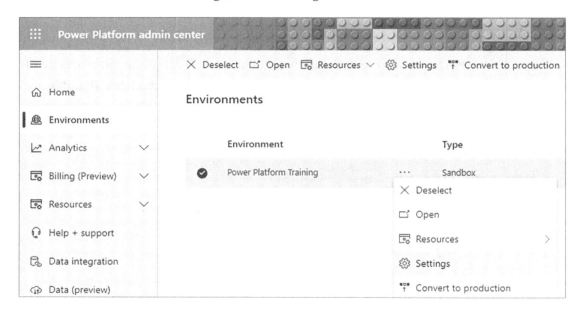

Figure 4-18. *Accessing environment settings in the Admin Center*

Once in the environment settings, either search for "Access Team Templates" or navigate to Templates and select "Access Team Templates," as seen in Figure 4-19.

Figure 4-19. *Access team templates settings*

Once in the access team templates settings, select "New" from the top control bar, as seen in Figure 4-20.

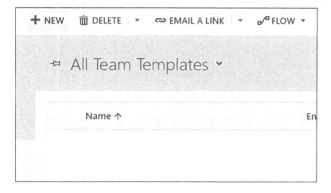

Figure 4-20. *Create new access team*

Once the Access Team Template dialogue shows up, you can begin filling out the fields to create your access team, as shown in Figure 4-21.

Figure 4-21. *Configure New Access Team dialogue*

The following attributes will need to be filled out to create your access team:

- **Name**: This is the display name for your auto-created access team.

Note   It is a good idea to include the table name and the general permissions in the name so you can easily distinguish this team from others. Example: Device Orders – Read Only

---

- **Entity**: This allows you to select the table to which you want to apply the access team. This means whenever a new record is created on this table, a new access team will be available for that record using this template.

Note   If your table is not listed here, it means that the table is not configured for access teams. Go to the table settings and enable "Have an access team" as seen in the beginning of this section.

- **Access Rights**: Here you configure the privileges of users who are added to the access team. The options include Delete, Append, Append To, Assign, Share, Read, and Write.

Business Units

Business units (BUs) allow users and teams to be organized in a hierarchy to allow cascading permissions based on who owns records. For instance, you might want to allow a team to work on records that are submitted by others on their team, or a manager to view all the records submitted by their subordinates' team members. Assigning your users and teams to business units and organizing those business units into logical hierarchies can reduce the need for users to manage permissions for their work and reduce the opportunity for data's being accessed or modified by the wrong people.

Business Unit Hierarchy

One key piece of information to keep in mind when thinking about your BU hierarchy is that a user can be assigned to one and only one BU at a time. This can create complications if a user needs to access data from two BUs that are at the same level, meaning that one is not a parent to the other. Whether or not you have this sort of requirement will dictate your type of permissions structure. Figure 4-22 shows a typical hierarchy model with a single organization and three divisions under that organization.

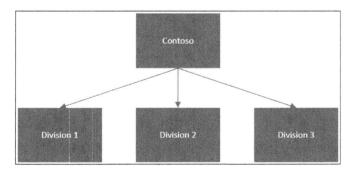

Figure 4-22. *Business unit hierarchy example*

There are two distinct types of security structures to be aware of when planning your design: hierarchical and matrix.

Hierarchical Security Model

The hierarchical model is ideal for organizations where a user works on contacts within their own BU or child BUs. Since a user can be assigned to one and only one business unit, a user can be granted permissions to view/work on contacts in their own BU. For instance, as illustrated in Figure 4-23, if a user is assigned to the Division A business unit, they would be able to work on contacts owned by users in Division A but not those in the other BUs. This can also be true if the user is assigned to the Contoso BU. However, since Contoso is a parent to Division A and Division B, the user could get access to the contacts in both Division A and Division B. The access to child BU records depends on the role that the user is given, so this distinction is customizable.

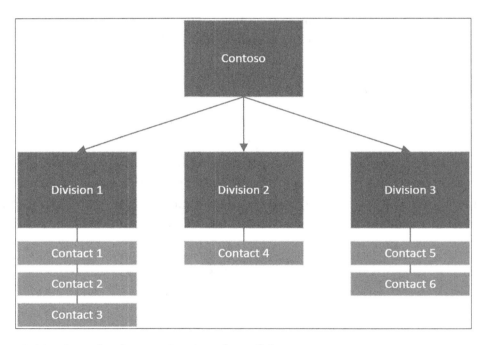

Figure 4-23. *Standard organizational model structure*

For business units (BUs) to be utilized to their fullest extent, it is important to organize them in a logical manner that allows for a cascade of permissions. While most people tend to model their BUs after their organizational reporting hierarchy, this is not always the best method because a user may report to one team but work on projects on another team. In this case, it may make more sense to assign that user to the BU of the team that they are working with.

However, it is not possible to give a user in the Contoso BU access to ONLY Division A contacts and not Division B records, because the configuration for roles applies to ALL child BUs, not specific child BUs. If this is a requirement for your implementation, you will want to look at the other permission model, which is called a matrix model.

Matrix Security Model

The matrix security model, also referred to as Modernized Business Units, is more complex in design and requires a more complicated management structure, but it allows more advanced permissions. For example, compared to the hierarchical security model where a user cannot be granted access to the contact records in Division A and Division B without also being granted access to the records in Division C, you can do exactly that in a matrix model. This is doable because you are no longer relying on the user's assigned business unit to determine where they are granted access. Instead, in a matrix model, the security roles specify which business unit they apply to. So, instead of assigning a user to a business unit, then a security role to that user, and letting the intersection of the two determine the user's access, you can create security roles that target a business unit directly and assign that security role to the user. You can also apply multiple security roles to a single user, and each security role can specify a different business unit. This allows you to set a different permissions level, and decide the extent of those permissions, at a very granular level and not have to worry about the constraints of the hierarchy model.

Referring back to Figure 4-23, assume you have the following requirements for a user:

- Edit all records in Division 1

- Read all records in Contoso

- Read all records in child business units of Contoso

- Read, edit, and delete records in Division 3

You would not be able to accomplish these security requirements in a hierarchy model, because the permissions for Divisions 1, 2, and 3 are all different. However, by using a matrix model, you can create a separate security role that targets each division and assign those roles to the user.

Note   If a hierarchical model is implemented and the business decides that a more complex matrix structure is required, the matrix feature can be enabled to allow the more complex security model to be utilized.

Business Units from Azure AD

Business units from Azure AD are a common implementation in organizations that already have Azure AD security groups set up or prefer to use Azure to manage groups. This model syncs the team and its users from the Azure group to the Dataverse group, where you can assign security roles and business groups, as seen in Figure 4-24.

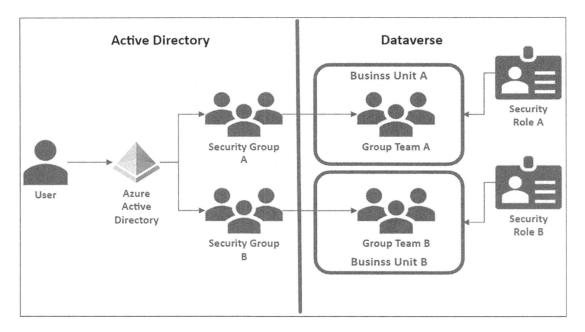

Figure 4-24.   *Business units from Azure AD security structure*

Cascading Permissions in Business Unit Permissions

Let's look at a few examples of how a hierarchical security model works that can help you get started.

In Figure 4-25, you can see that a user is assigned to Division 1. At this level, if a user is given Parent:Child Business Units scope for permissions for the Contact table, they will be able to operate on contacts within Division 1.

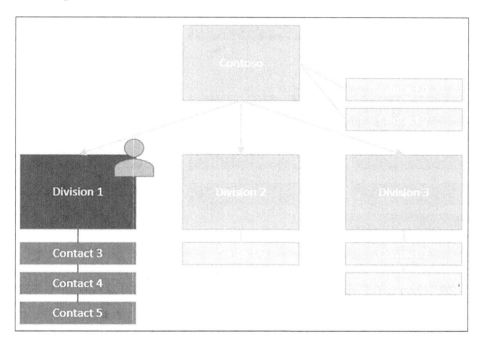

Figure 4-25. *User with child business unit assigned*

If the user were to be reassigned to the Contoso, or parent, business unit level, then the permissions would allow them to operate on Contoso contacts, as well as all the contact records owned by the child business units of Contoso (Figure 4-26).

101

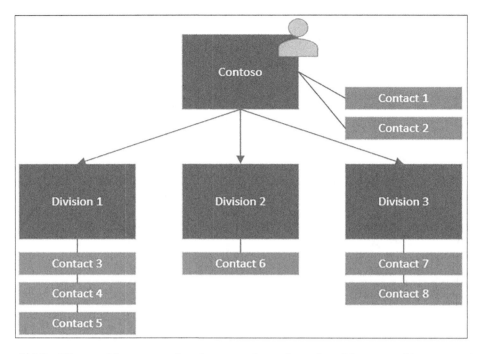

Figure 4-26. *User with parent business unit assigned, with cascading permissions*

If you were to keep the user at the same level, but change the permission scope to be Business Unit instead of Parent:Child Business Units, they would only be able to operate on records owned by the Contoso business and nothing below it. An illustration of this concept can be seen in Figure 4-27.

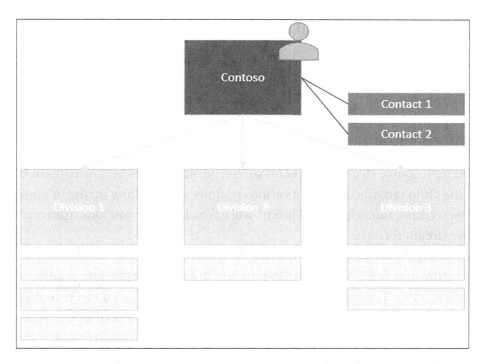

Figure 4-27. *User with Parent Business Unit assigned, without cascading permissions*

Record Inheritance

Record inheritance allows permissions to be passed from a parent record to a child record across the relationships between them. For instance, you may want a user who has edit rights to a project record to automatically have edit rights to the activities that are related to that project, but not activities that are unrelated to that project. This can make managing records a lot easier because you can manage the permissions for the parent record, and the child records are automatically managed for you. It can also make your data more secure because it avoids the need for sharing records at different levels, which can cause a lot of segmented permissions that are difficult to audit. In general, the more you can rely on well-structured security models, the less users need to share records directly, which means less segmentation of permissions.

Considerations for Inheritance

There are several things to consider when designing your record inheritance structure to ensure that your model behaves the way you expect it to, and that data isn't inadvertently accessible or lost.

Permissions Flow Downstream

The record inheritance structure is set up so that permissions flow downstream from the parent to the child records. There are various options when setting up the relationship type between tables, but selecting "Parent" will cascade all permissions from one record to the downstream records.

If you use Figure 4-28 as an example, let's say that the top-level relationships, indicated by the number 1, were set to Parent, but the lower-level relationships, indicated by number 2, were set to Referential. In this example, if you were to delete the project record, it would also delete both Release 1 and Release 2 records because any action taken to the parent record is carried over to the child records. However, since the level 2 relationship is only a referential type of relationship, it will not remove the feature records. The feature records would remain in the system and would simply not be associated with any release records. The feature records would essentially be orphan records since they would no longer be associated with a record structure.

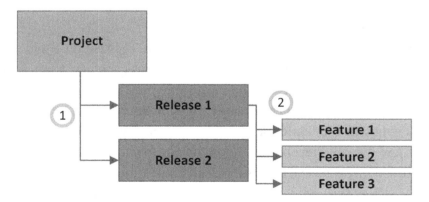

Figure 4-28. *Table relationship permissions example*

While there are cases where removing the parent records is desired, such as when a record has more than one parent record and you want to keep the record for the sake of the other relationship, it is wise to keep your data clean by avoiding orphaned records caused by removing a parent record but not the child. Depending on how you have the relationships set up, you may or may not be able to delete the parent record while there are child records assigned to it. If you have configured the relationships to not be parental, or not restrict delete, then you will be able to delete the parent records without first deleting or reassigning the child records. This is why it is good to have one relationship set as Parental or configured to restrict delete when there is a practical parent/child relationship between tables, instead of simply a referential relationship.

One Parent Relationship per Table

While you can configure your database to have multiple parents in a hierarchical sense, you can only have one relationship defined as a parent relationship. This restriction prevents circular loops of permissions and logic. If you attempt to set up a second parental relationship when one already exists for a table, you will be given a warning message, as seen in Figure 4-29.

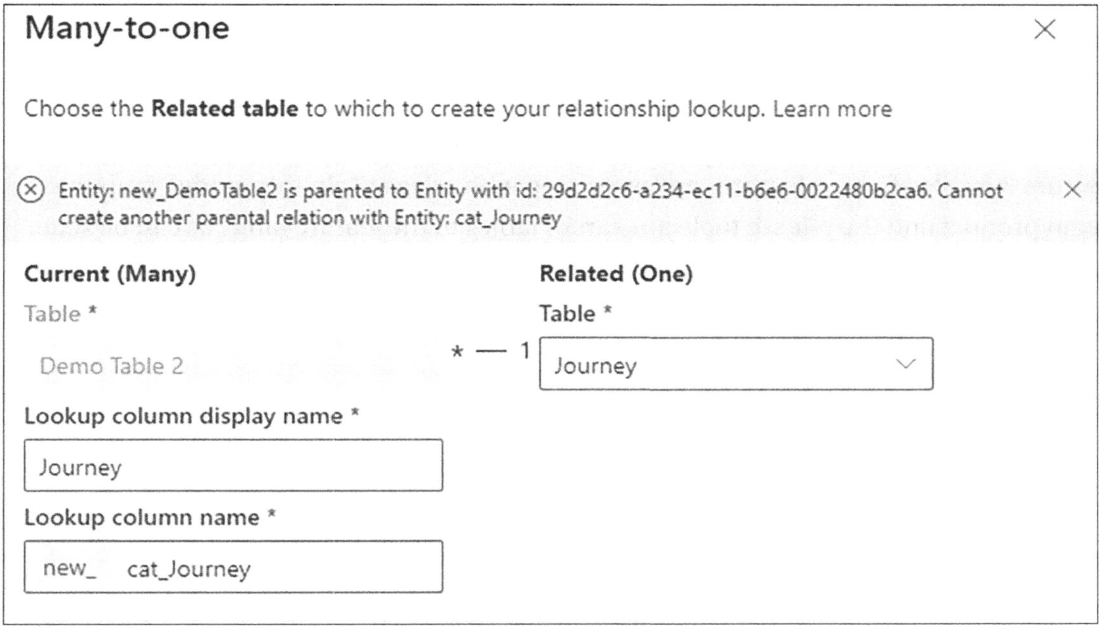

Figure 4-29. *Multiple parent relationships error*

This is another reason it is best to plan your data structure carefully, so you don't run into this issue down the road. Fortunately, there are ways around this, as follows:

1. Relationships can be removed after they are created. So, in the case where a relationship is created by error, it can always be removed. Keep in mind, however, that removing a relationship can result in lost data since doing so will remove any foreign key values that associate that record with its parent record. It may be obvious once you think about it, but I have seen makers restructure relationships without thinking about the data impacts. This brings us to the next option.

2. Relationships can be modified. Often the architecture issues are simply due to the wrong type of relationship being set up. Fortunately, you can change a relationship behavior type after it is created. By switching a relationship from parent to referential, you can ensure that your records are still related, and you can navigate between them, but it allows you to create a parent relationship to another table if you need to inherit permissions from a different table.

An example of why you may want multiple parent tables for a record is illustrated in Figure 4-30. Here you can see how a feature may be related to a release, but also be related to a product. The product may be associated with feature 1 and feature 2, but not feature 3, while all three features are associated with release 1. In this model, both the team product and the release table are parent tables to the feature table, as can be seen by the direction of the one-to-many relationship. However, only one of the relationships can be parental due to circular logic restrictions.

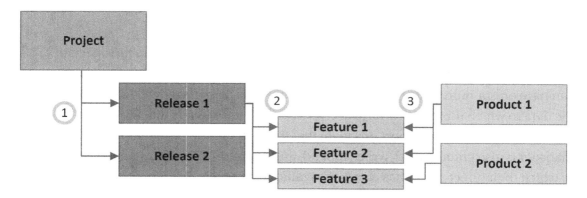

Figure 4-30. *Multiple parent table model*

In this model, you would have to decide if relationship 2 or relationship 3 is the parent or if neither is a parent and they are both referential. An argument can be made for all three cases, and it depends on how you want your data to act.

Hierarchy Security

Hierarchy security allows users to be organized in a hierarchical manner so that a user has access to data that the users who are below them on the hierarchy have access to. This feature can be used in conjunction with other security features to further automate the security model, primarily reducing the number of business units that are required to organize data.

Note   Users who have their account status set as Disabled are excluded from the hierarchy security model, and their records will not be available to the users higher in the hierarchy.

There are two types of hierarchy security models: manager and position. With a manager hierarchy, the manager must be in the same business unit as their direct report (employee) or within the parent business unit of the direct report's business unit, whereas with position hierarchy, data can be accessed from business units. Deciding which method works for you will depend on if you want to segment your data by business unit or not.

Manager Hierarchy

The manager hierarchy utilizes the Manager field on the system user table to dictate the reporting structure. Each user can have one and only one manager, but a manager can have one or more direct reports. Within this model, a manager will have access to the data to which their reports have access. This includes records that are owned by or shared with the direct report or a team that the direct report is a member of. The manager is also granted read, write, append, and append-to privileges for any records to which their direct report has access. This allows managers to not only see what work their direct report is doing, but also perform work on behalf of their direct report.

Note   For a manager to have access to a direct report's records on a table, the manager must have at least read-level access to a table or they will not be able to see the records of their direct report.

For non-direct reports in the same management chain, the manager has read-only access to the data of the users below them. This can be further explained using Figure 4-31 as an example.

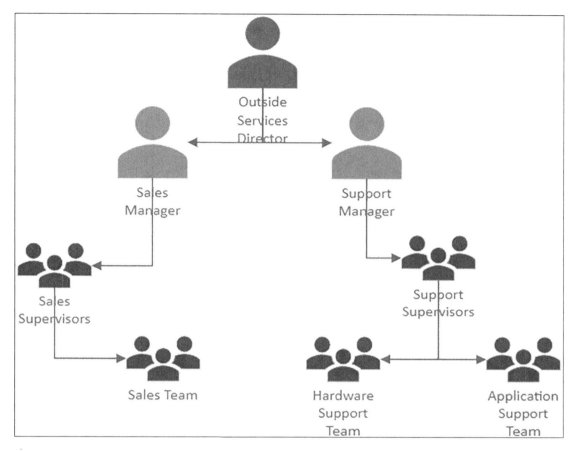

Figure 4-31. *Sample manager hierarchy structure*

In this example, the support manager will have read, write, append, and append-to rights on any records that either support supervisor has access to. However, support supervisor 1 will have read only access to the records of the hardware support team users and application support team users. The same applies if you move one layer up, where the director will have read, write, append, and append-to rights on both managers' records but have read-only access to the supervisor's records.

There is also a depth setting in the hierarchy security settings that allows you to specify how deep the permissions go. For example, if the depth setting is set to 2, then the director will have access to the manager- and supervisor-level users' records, but not the support- and sales-level records.

Position Hierarchy

Position hierarchy is not based on reporting structure, but rather on positions that are set up and assigned to users. The positions are arranged in a hierarchy, and the users that are assigned those positions inherit permissions through the hierarchy of those positions, as seen in Figure 4-32.

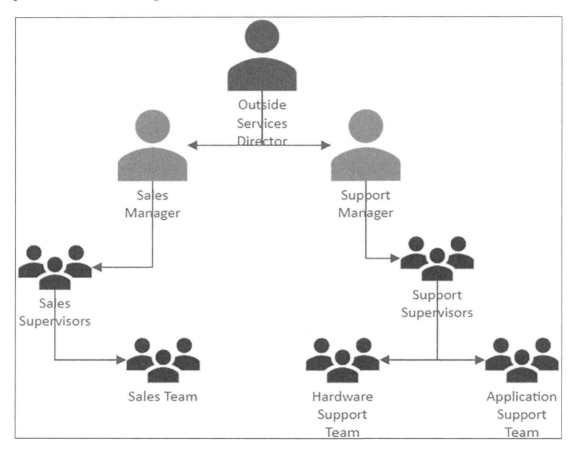

Figure 4-32. *Sample position hierarchy tructure*

A user can have only one position, but a position can be assigned to multiple users. Similarly, a position can have only one parent position, but multiple positions can be assigned to a single parent position. This allows for building a pyramid-style structure like that of the manager hierarchy model. However, unlike the manager hierarchy model, since users are not reporting to other users, users can be organized across multiple business units. This allows for a more flexible security design for users to work in a structure, like a support team where a manager can have team members working across multiple business units.

If you compare Figure 4-31 and Figure 4-32, you will see that the same users are structured differently. This is because in a position hierarchy, users are structured using positions, not reporting managers. This means that all the support supervisors are lumped together and the hardware support team reports to the group of support supervisors instead of a specific support supervisor. The same applies to the sales team and sales supervisors because they have been "tagged" with the same position.

The permissions cascade is the same as the manager hierarchy, where the director has read, write, append, and append-to rights on both managers' records, or any records of their associated teams, but read-only rights on the levels below that to the extent the depth setting allows.

Because the positions are not assigned business units and users are not assigned to report to a specific user, it is now easy to see how access can be organized across multiple business units. An application support team can have users that span multiple business units, and the support supervisors will retain their inherited permissions from all the records that the users in positions that are below their own position have access to.

Setting Up Hierarchy Security

To set up hierarchy security, you will go to the Power Platform Admin Center and access the settings for your environment. From there you will select "Hierarchy security" under the User + Permissions section, as shown in Figure 4-33.

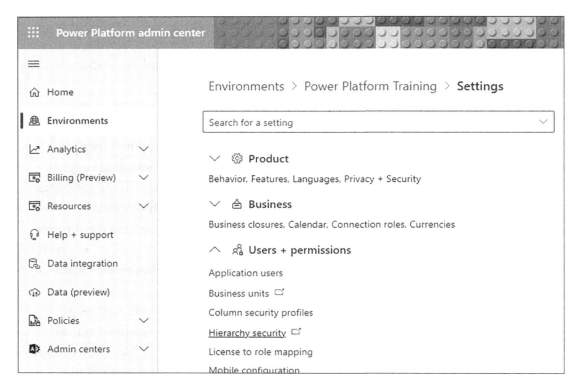

Figure 4-33. *Accessing hierarchy security settings*

Next, you will set up the basics of the hierarchy security, as seen in Figure 4-34.

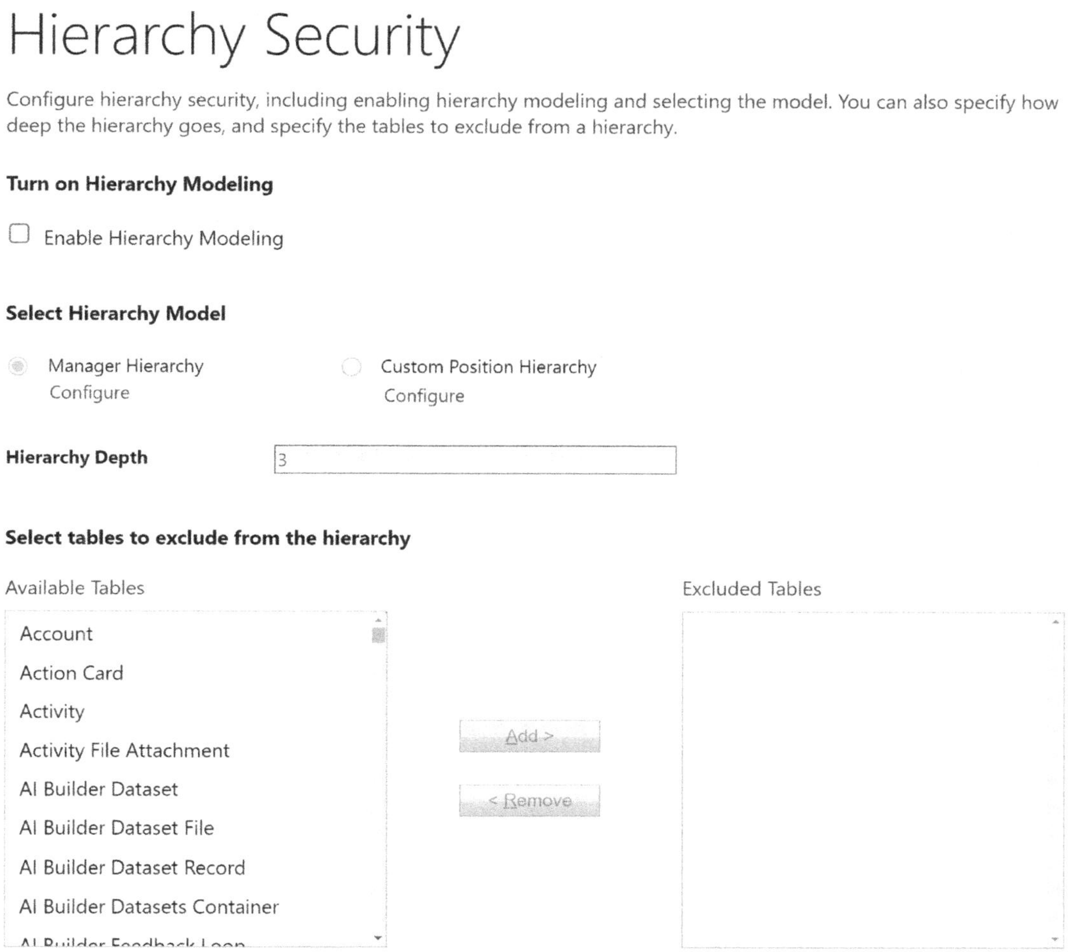

Hierarchy Security

Configure hierarchy security, including enabling hierarchy modeling and selecting the model. You can also specify how deep the hierarchy goes, and specify the tables to exclude from a hierarchy.

Turn on Hierarchy Modeling

☐ Enable Hierarchy Modeling

Select Hierarchy Model

◉ Manager Hierarchy
   Configure

◯ Custom Position Hierarchy
   Configure

Hierarchy Depth   3

Select tables to exclude from the hierarchy

Available Tables

Account
Action Card
Activity
Activity File Attachment
AI Builder Dataset
AI Builder Dataset File
AI Builder Dataset Record
AI Builder Datasets Container
AI Builder Feedback Loop

Excluded Tables

Add >

< Remove

Figure 4-34. *Hierarchy Security settings dialogue*

- **Turn on Hierarchy Modeling**: Check this box to enable this feature.

- **Select Hierarchy Model**: Select the type of security model you want to use.

- **Hierarchy Depth**: Specify the number of levels that the hierarchy security will traverse.

- **Select tables to exclude from the hierarchy**: Move any tables that you do not want to be included in the hierarchy security model to the "Excluded Tables" section. Otherwise, all tables are included in the model by default.

Next, you will want to configure your hierarchy model. The method of configuration for this depends on the model you choose.

Configuring Manager Hierarchy

For the manager hierarchy model, select "Configure" under the Manager Hierarchy option in the hierarchy security configuration window in Figure 4-34. A window will open with a list of users to select managers for, as seen in Figure 4-35.

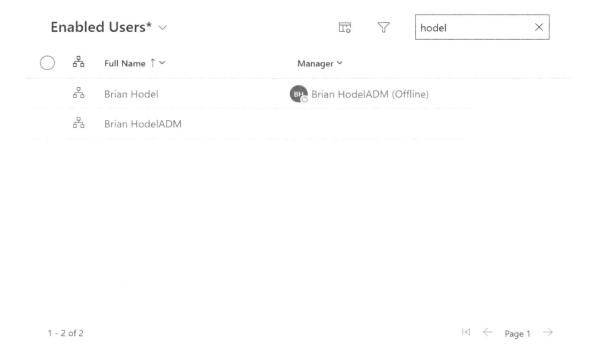

Figure 4-35. *Manager hierarchy configuration screen*

Note   If you do not see the Manager field in this view, click the Edit Columns button and add it to the view.

Here, you will proceed to either select the user's managers, or you can populate these by loading an Excel template, which you can download and upload by clicking the Excel Templates button in the top control bar, as seen in Figure 4-36.

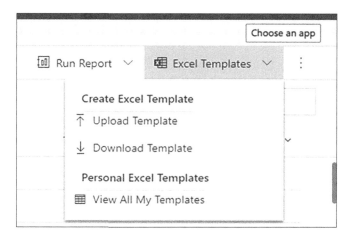

Figure 4-36. *Excel Templates settings flyout*

Additionally, you can populate this using flows or apps or in various other ways, but, essentially, you will need the Manager field populated for any users who are going to participate in the hierarchy security.

Configuring Position Hierarchy

For the position hierarchy, select "Configure" under the Custom Position Hierarchy in the hierarchy security configuration window. A window will open up with a list of positions, as seen in Figure 4-37.

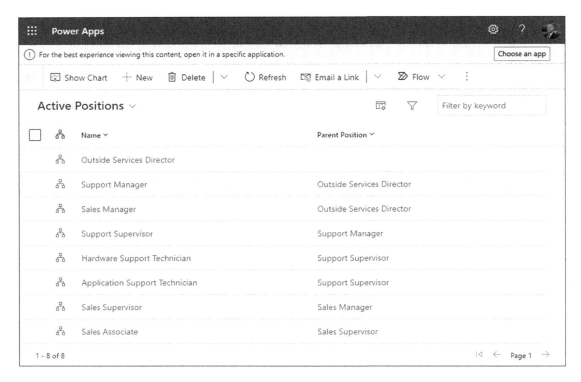

Figure 4-37. *Position hierarchy configuration screen*

To add a new position, select "+New" from the top command bar. A new form opens, as seen in Figure 4-38.

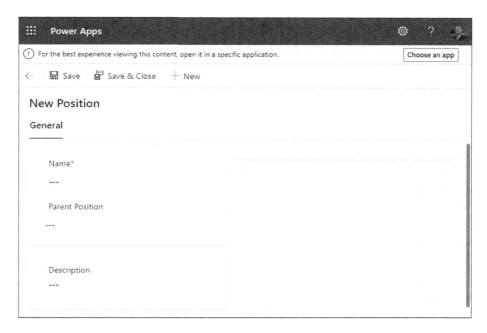

Figure 4-38. *New Position form*

Enter a name for the position and select a parent position from the dropdown. You can also add a description to help identify the purpose of the role.

After clicking Save in the top control bar, the form will change to allow the addition of users to the position, as seen in Figure 4-39.

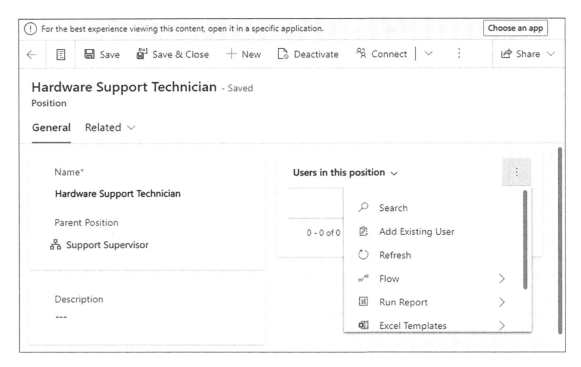

Figure 4-39. *Adding users to new position*

Once you are done with the configuration of this section, be sure to click Save and Close from the top control bar of the hierarchy security window to apply your new security model.

Column Security Profiles

Another common security scenario in database design is column-level security. In Dataverse, this is accomplished with column security profiles. Column security profiles allow columns to be restricted to certain users or groups of users. This feature can be useful in a situation where you have users accessing records that have sensitive data in certain columns, such as a pay rate or Social Security number. Security profiles can be configured for groups of fields or individual fields.

Setting Up Column Security

To enable column-level security, navigate to the table that has the column that needs a column security profile added to it. Open the columns list, select the ellipse next to the column you want to edit, then select "Edit" from the menu, as seen in Figure 4-40.

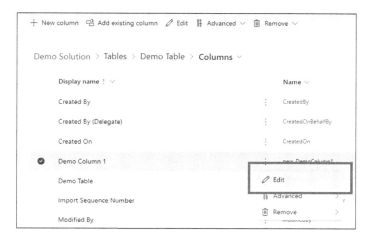

Figure 4-40. *Editing column settings*

Once the column settings flyout opens, select "Advanced Options" and check "Enable Column Security," then click Save to apply changes, as seen in Figure 4-41.

Figure 4-41. *Enabling column security for a selected column*

This enables the column for column-level security but does not yet specify who can interact with the column.

Creating the Column Security Profile

To create the security profile, open the solution and select New ➤ Security ➤ Column Security Profile, as seen in Figure 4-42.

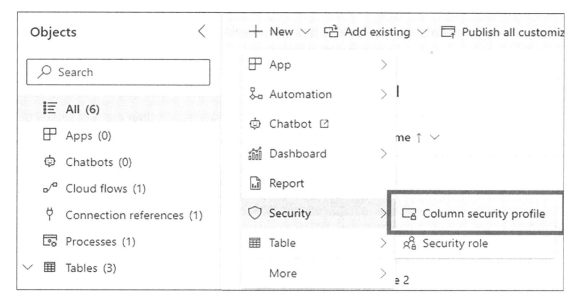

Figure 4-42. *Selecting new column security profile inside solution*

A dialogue will open asking for name and description, as shown in Figure 4-43.

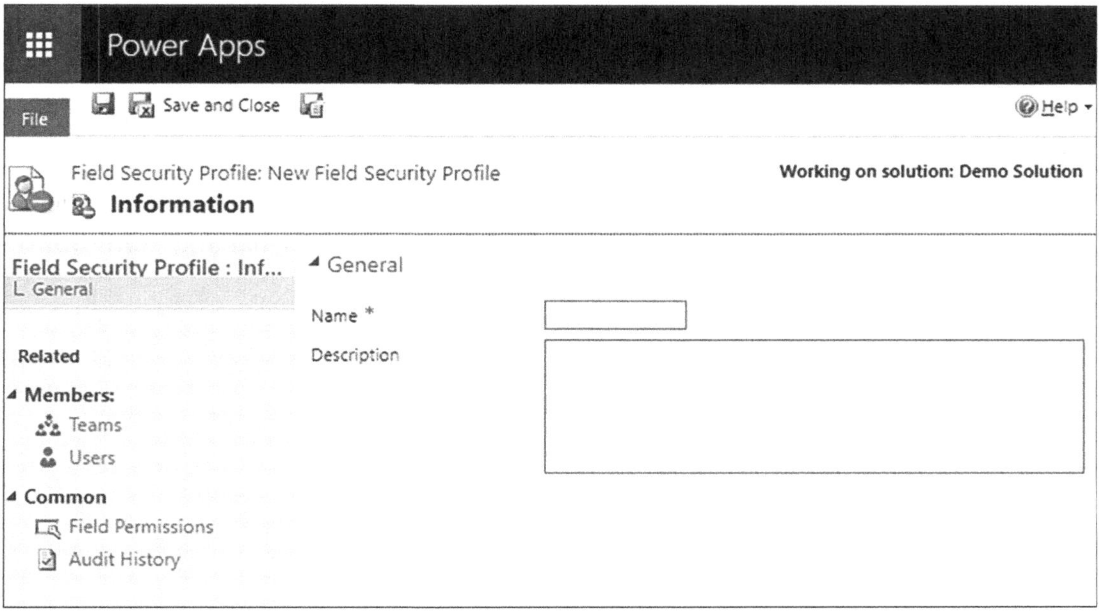

Figure 4-43. *Field security profile creation form*

Note   The term *field security profile* has been replaced by *column security profile* as Microsoft has moved to their Unified Interface model. Until the migration is complete, the terms can be used interchangeably.

Once the Name and, optionally, Description, fields have been filled out, click Save in the upper control ribbon to create the security profile, as seen in Figure 4-44.

Figure 4-44. *Clicking Save button in Field Security Profile form*

Adding Users and Teams to Profile

Once the security profile has been created, the sidebar options will be made available. This section will allow the addition of users and/or teams to the security profile, as well as allow adjustments to field permissions and review of the audit history of the profile.

To add teams to the profile, select "Teams" from the left control bar and "Add" from the top control bar, as seen in Figure 4-45.

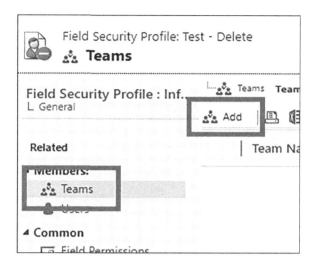

Figure 4-45. *Opening teams lookup dialogue*

This will open a Look Up Records dialogue where teams can be searched for and added to the security profile. Simply select the teams you wish to add by checking the box next to each, then click the Select button, as seen in Figure 4-46. Once you are done, select "Add," and the teams will be added to your security profile.

123

Figure 4-46. *Adding teams to security profile*

To add individual users to the security profile, do the same steps as outlined for adding teams, but select "Users" in the first step instead.

Configuring Field Permissions

To configure the permissions for the security profile, select "Field Permissions" from the left-hand navigation bar. A list of the fields that have been set as having column security enabled will be displayed, as seen in Figure 4-47. The list shows the field name, display name, and entity (table), as well as several other attributes of the field to ensure you are selecting the correct field to configure.

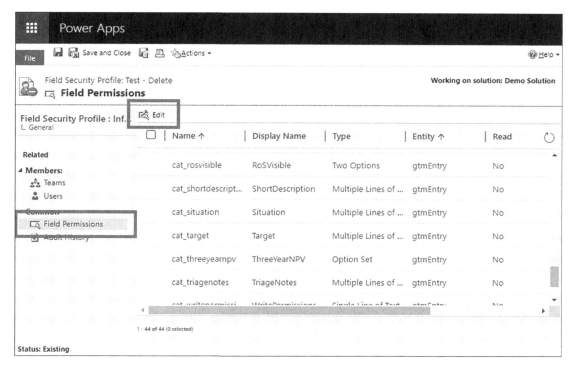

Figure 4-47. Configuring field permissions

Select the row of the field you wish to adjust permissions for and select "Edit," as seen in Figure 4-47. A dialogue will open to edit the field security settings of the selected field, as seen in Figure 4-48. Here, you can configure whether the members of the security profile can read, update, and/or create data in the field. To add another column to the security profile, simply select another field and configure it like the previous one. A single profile can have multiple columns configured in it, and a single column can be configured for multiple security profiles. This is another reason to use the description field when creating profiles—so you can understand the implications of applying a field security profile to a user/team and easily troubleshoot security issues if they arise.

Figure 4-48. *Edit Field Security dialogue*

Click OK when done, then Save and Close to apply changes.

Auditing

Dataverse's auditing capabilities are extensive and allow you to monitor actions such as system access, setting updates, and data changes. The auditing capabilities are also highly customizable so you can adjust what is audited and how those logs are maintained.

Enabling Auditing

By default, an environment's auditing is disabled, so no audit data is collected. To enable auditing, go to the Power Platform Admin Center and select your environment to open the environment settings summary screen. From there, find the Auditing section, as seen in Figure 4-49.

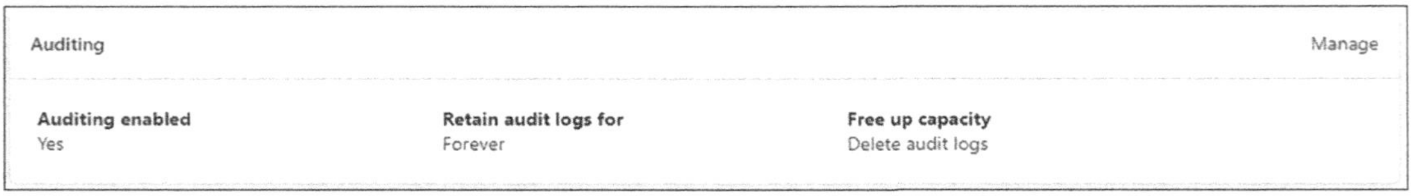

Figure 4-49. *Environmental auditing settings status display*

You can see the status of the environment's auditing settings here. If Auditing Enabled is set to No, select "Manage" to open the Auditing settings for the environment. This will open a new form, as seen in Figure 4-50, where you will be able to enable and configure auditing.

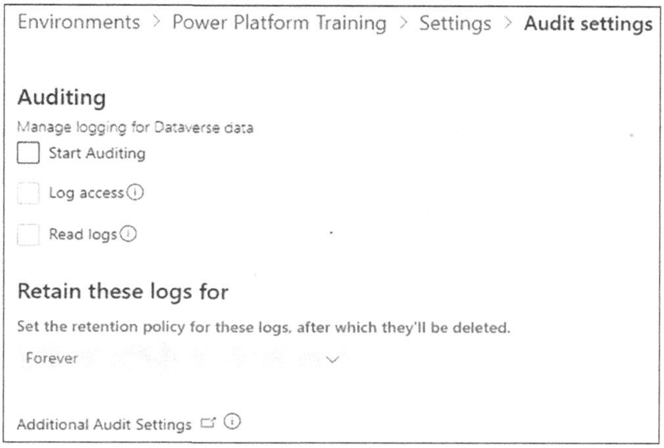

Figure 4-50. *Environment auditing settings configuration*

The options here are as follows:

- **Start Auditing**: Enable auditing functionality in the environment. This is the base setting to enable any logging at all and must be enabled to log any level of the Dataverse environment.

- **Log Access**: Enable auditing of users accessing the environment, generally by signing in.

- **Read Logs**: Sends audit logs to Microsoft Purview for review and analysis functionality in addition to the default audit log review functionality in Dataverse.

- **Retain These Logs For**: Specifies how long the audit logs will be retained. Since there is a cost to all data storage, including audit logs, it is good to evaluate how long you want audit data to be retained in your system.

Advanced Audit Settings

Additional settings can be configured in the legacy Dynamics 365 settings page by selecting "Additional Audit Settings," as seen on the bottom of Figure 4-50. Once the new window opens, select the menu arrow next to Settings on the top control bar, as seen in Figure 4-51.

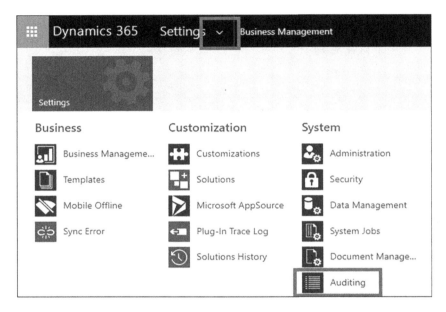

Figure 4-51. *Selecting auditing in legacy admin interface*

Note   This interface looks a bit different because it is still in the legacy design Dynamics 365 interface as not all features have been migrated to the new Unified Interface as of the writing of this book.

Once in the advanced audit settings screen, you will be able to access advanced audit log configuration settings, as well as the audit summary view, as seen in Figure 4-52.

Figure 4-52. *Advanced audit settings screen*

Selecting "Audit Summary View" displays a list of all the audit log entries for your environment. To filter the entries, select "Enable/Disable Filters," as seen in Figure 4-53.

Changed Date ↓	Event	Changed By	User Info	Record	Entity	Operation
1/14/2023 2:07 PM	User Access via Web	SYSTEM		Hodel, Brian	User	Access
1/14/2023 2:07 PM	User Access via Web	SYSTEM		Hodel, Brian	User	Access
1/14/2023 2:06 PM	User Access via Web	SYSTEM		Flow-RP, #	User	Access
1/14/2023 2:06 PM	User Access via Web	SYSTEM		Flow-RP, #	User	Access
1/14/2023 2:01 PM	User Access via Web	SYSTEM		Flow-CDSNative	User	Access
1/14/2023 1:20 PM	User Access via Web	SYSTEM		CDSUserManag	User	Access
1/14/2023 1:20 PM	User Access via Web	SYSTEM		CDSFileStorage,	User	Access

Figure 4-53. *Audit Summary View*

Note   Only the legacy audit log interface is discussed in this section because the new Purview integration is not yet available as of the writing of this book.

129

Enabling Auditing of Tables

To audit data changes in a table, the Audit setting must be enabled for each table in the table properties.

To do this, navigate to the table properties for the table that needs to have auditing enabled and check the "Audit changes to its data" option, as seen in Figure 4-54, then click Save. This will begin auditing the data for that table.

Primary row image

None

Refine how data in this table is used and managed. Op
enabled. Learn more

For this table

☑ Apply duplicate detection rules ⓘ

☑ Track changes [1] ⓘ

☐ Provide custom help ⓘ

Help URL

Log any data creation, changes, or deletion in ✕
this table. When turned on, all columns are
audited by default.

Won't run if auditing is turned off for your
environment

Learn more

☑ Audit changes to its data ⓘ

☐ Leverage quick-create form if
available ⓘ

☐ Enable Archival ⓘ

Figure 4-54.   Enabling audit in table settings

If auditing is not enabled for the environment, a warning will appear below the checkbox stating that no data will be audited until auditing is enabled for the environment, as seen in Figure 4-55. The option can still be enabled, but no audit data will be collected until environment-level auditing is enabled.

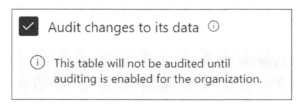

☑ Audit changes to its data ⓘ

ⓘ This table will not be audited until
auditing is enabled for the organization.

Figure 4-55.   Table settings warning if environment-level auditing is not enabled

Summary

As you can see, there are many ways to apply security to the Dataverse data, and the ability to layer those security methods can create a very complex array of security options. This can be a great asset in your toolbox for building solutions, but can also be very troublesome if it is not configured correctly. This is why it is important to always plan your architecture carefully and document as you go so your solutions are robust as well as resilient. Next, you will learn how to display the data to your users by building reports and apps.

CHAPTER 5

Presentation Layer

In the previous chapter, we discussed the Security Layer and how to utilize the advanced security features in Dataverse, such as Teams, Business Units, and auditing, to ensure data is secure. In this chapter, we discuss the Presentation Layer which consists of various methods of presenting and interacting with your data. In Power Platform, there are several tools with which to do this, such as Power Apps, Power BI, and Power Pages. Designing an interface for your data is one of the more challenging aspects of designing a solution because it is where users interact with data. It needs to be built in such a way that users can intuitively find and navigate data structures. In my experience, this part of the process involves numerous iterations to find a balance between functionality and what makes sense to users.

The tool you choose depends on the audience, user account type, type of data interaction, and various other factors. Choosing the correct tool, or tools, for the job is imperative not only to build an effective tool, but also to ensure user adoption is smooth and successful.

Apps

Applications, typically referred to as apps, are visual representations of data. Typically, end users do not understand terms like *schema*, *foreign keys*, and *attributes*, and they should not have to. You would never expect a project manager to go into a database and start updating the project status by writing SQL statements, or a director to look at project budgets by running queries in SQL Server Management Studio. Neither of these users would likely have the skill set or bandwidth to do such things. Also, to do this type of work, the user would have to know the tables, relationships, attributes, and so on to even start. This is why we have apps—to make accessing and interacting with data simple and intuitive. In fact, I use the amount of training and support required to gauge how effective an app is. If users can go into an app and quickly learn how to use it and

133

B. Hodel, *Beginning Microsoft Dataverse*, https://doi.org/10.1007/978-1-4842-9334-8_5

get the information that they need, then it is a good app. If extensive training is required and users struggle navigating the menus to find the information they need, then it is a bad app.

In Power Platform, there are multiple tools for developing apps, and each has its advantages and disadvantages, so it is good to familiarize yourself with each type to ensure you have the best tool for the outcome you seek. However, like the rest of the platform, it is common to have a mix of tools. Often, a canvas app will be deployed in parallel with a model-driven app and have different target audiences. I have often developed a model-driven app for administrative/advanced users who need to do very granular data manipulation but are not concerned with a "pretty" interface alongside a canvas app that is available to basic users and executives who need to be able to quickly go in and get what they need from the app but do not need to see all the details, as seen in Figure 5-1. However, there are many reasons to use each type and many capabilities of each that do overlap.

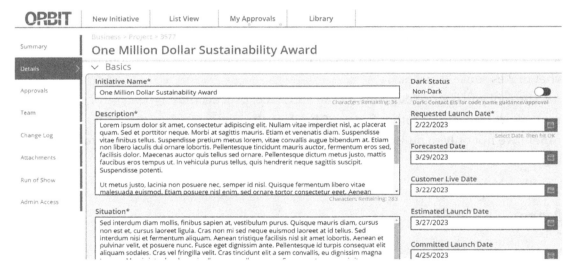

Figure 5-1. *Canvas app example*

Canvas Apps

Canvas apps allow the development of apps with nearly unlimited customization capability. While model-driven apps do allow for some customization and theming, canvas apps allow for pixel-perfect control over nearly every aspect of the app design, allowing layouts, colors, sizes, and fonts to be fully customized to meet the needs of your customers. Any limitations that do exist in the native app development tools can be accomplished using full-code components that can be integrated into the app.

User Interface Design

As you can see from the examples in Figure 5-2 and Figure 5-3, the layout and formatting can vary from one canvas app to the next. This is a positive in that an app can be designed to conform tightly to brand standards and reflect the data structure in a way that is intuitive to the users. However, the ability to configure the app design also means that the design can vary from one app to another, making it more challenging for users to transition from one app to another.

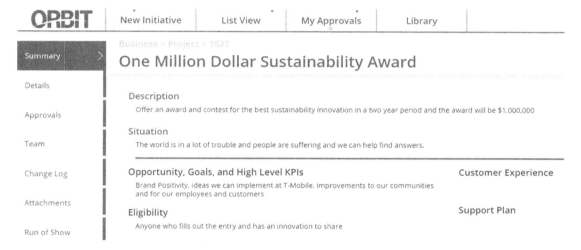

Figure 5-2. *Example 1 of canvas app design capabilities*

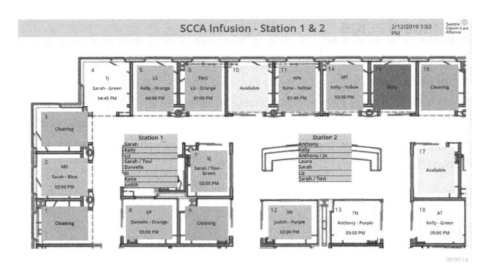

Figure 5-3. *Example 1 of canvas app design capabilities*

One way to address these concerns is to utilize components in your apps. Components are prebuilt UI (user interface) elements, or sets of elements, that are built by you and shared using component libraries. Things like navigation menus, dialogue windows, people pickers, and so forth can be built in your own style and published to a component library for use across any of the apps in your environment. Once a component is published to a component library, any app developer in the environment can import it to their app so that the set of elements is consistent and familiar to users. A good example of consistency in app design is Office. Word, Excel, and PowerPoint all follow very similar UI designs. Components also save a lot of time as these elements do not need to be rebuilt for every screen or app that is developed. In addition, when a change is made to a component in a component library, that change is available as an update to all the apps that have imported that component. This means that logos, fonts, colors, sizes, features, and so on can all be updated one time and simply be updated in each app by selecting the Update option when the app is opened in Edit mode.

Creating a Canvas App

The best way to create a canvas app is to go into your solution and select Create ➤ New ➤ Canvas App from the top toolbar, as seen in Figure 5-4.

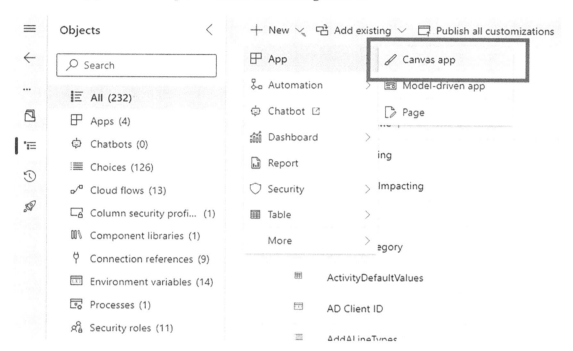

Figure 5-4. *Creating a new canvas app*

Note   Although these instructions outline creating a blank app, the creation of apps from templates is possible by going to Power Apps home and selecting "More Create Options." This can help you get started by seeing how controls are configured and interact before building one from scratch.

Once the app has opened, there will be a single blank screen. Being familiar with the Power Apps Studio layout for canvas apps will help you be more efficient while building your apps. Figure 5-5 maps out the various sections of Power Apps Studio.

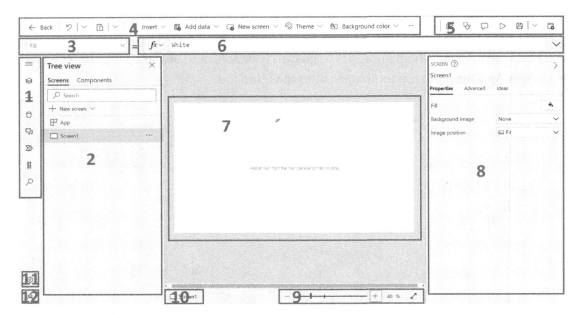

Figure 5-5. *Power Apps Studio layout*

Power Apps Studio comprises the following sections:

1. **App Authoring Menu**: List of app authoring categories, such as media, control menus, and tree view. Some of these properties are also available in the modern command bar.

2. **App Authoring Options**: Context menus for authoring menu selection. The tree view is an especially useful option to navigating levels of controls and containers.

3. **Properties List**: List of properties for selected control or screen

4. **Power Apps Studio Modern Command Bar**: Menus to add controls, data sources, and other development settings

5. **App Actions**: App save/publish, preview, app checker, and other settings

6. **Formula Bar**: Formula space for selected property

7. **Canvas / Screen**: Development canvas for app

8. **Properties Pane**: List of properties for the selected control or screen

9. **Zoom**: Zoom in / out and fit to screen

10. **Screen Selector**: List to easily switch between different screens

11. **Settings**: App, display, upcoming features, and support settings

12. **Virtual Agent Assistant**: Chatbot to assist with Power Apps questions

To get started, add a data source by selecting "Add Data" from the command bar. Select a Dataverse table, and it will be added to your app. The added table will also move from the Tables section to the In Your App section, as seen in Figure 5-6.

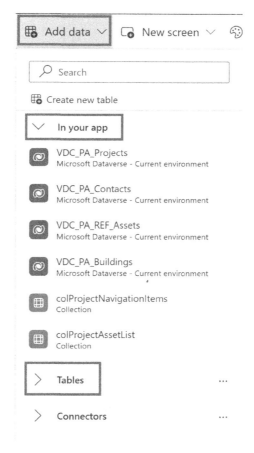

Figure 5-6. *Add Data menu in Power Apps Studio*

Note   Since Dataverse is the native data source for Power Apps, the tables in the environment are automatically connected to the app and available to be added without creating a connection. Other data sources require the additional step of setting up the connection, which varies depending on the connector.

Once you have a data source in your app, you can begin adding controls with which to interact with the data. The most common control in an app is the form control since it allows you to easily interact with data and requires little configuration to be functional.

To start, select "Insert" from the top command bar, and select "Edit Form," as seen in Figure 5-7.

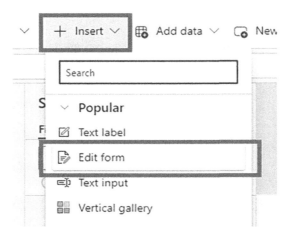

Figure 5-7. *Inserting form control*

Note   You can also access the control list by selecting "Insert" from the app authoring menu and selecting "Edit Form" from the app authoring options list. As the Power Apps tool has evolved, the interface has evolved, so you will see multiple options for performing the same task in a few places.

Once you have added the form control to the page, you will see a square that says, "This form is not connected to any data yet. Connect to data." Select the form control, and the Properties pane on the right will display the list of properties for the control. Select the "Data Source" menu from the Properties pane and select the table you want the form to interact with, as seen in Figure 5-8.

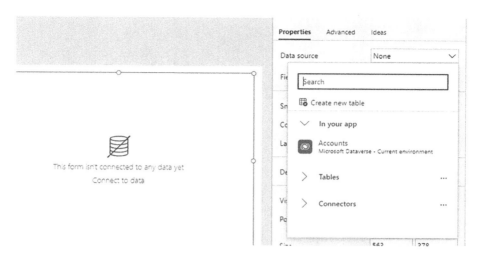

Figure 5-8. *Selecting data source for form control*

Once you have selected the table, Power Apps will begin setting up your form by adding fields to it. If you want to adjust the fields by adding or removing fields, select "Edit Fields" from the Properties pane, as seen in Figure 5-9.

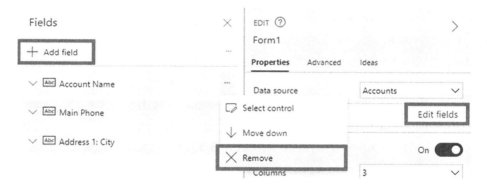

Figure 5-9. *Adding or removing fields from form control*

The next step is to set the form mode to New instead of the default of Edit since we want to create a new record. To do this, select the form control, then select "Advanced" in the Properties pane. Find the "Data" section and start typing "FormMode.New" in the DefaultMode field. As you type, you can see that predictive text suggests text to complete the formula, which makes it much easier to format your formulas correctly, as seen in Figure 5-10.

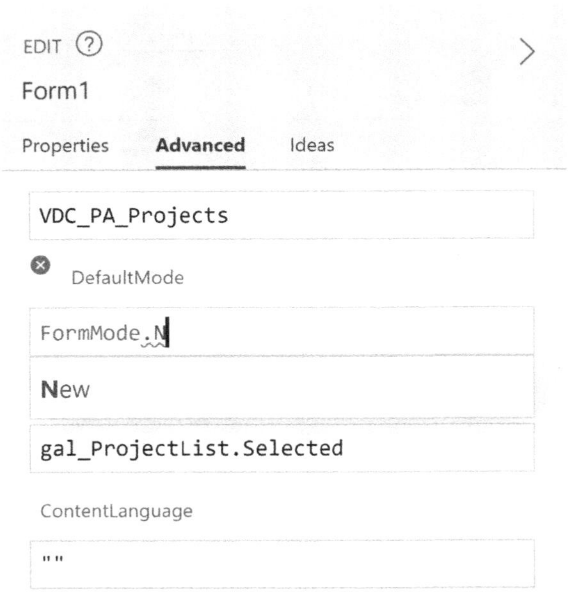

EDIT ⑦   >

Form1

Properties   **Advanced**   Ideas

VDC_PA_Projects

⊗ DefaultMode

FormMode.N

New

gal_ProjectList.Selected

ContentLanguage

" "

Figure 5-10. *Predictive text for formulas*

Note   You can also use the formula bar by selecting "DefaultMode" from the properties list then typing the formula into the formula bar.

Form controls are groups of controls instead of controls themselves. You can see the layers of controls in the tree view of the App Authoring Options pane after selecting the tree view app-authoring menu, as seen in Figure 5-11. This view is especially useful for seeing how your controls are layered and grouped on the page.

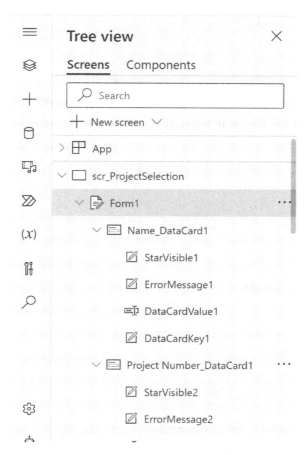

Figure 5-11. *Tree view of form control*

Each control has its own set of properties and can be configured independently. However, Power Apps does this automatically when inserting a form to make the process faster.

As you can see in Figure 5-11, each control has a unique name. These names are important for formulas, so you can rename them by selecting the ellipses next to the control in the tree view and rename them to something useful.

Note   Using a naming convention for your controls helps to keep things organized. I prefer to use three letters that refer to the type of control, an underscore, then a description of the control, such as frm_NewAccountForm for a new account form control.

The next step is to add a button control to submit the form. To do this, add a new control to the form and place it where you want it on the page. You can change the text on the button, along with many other aspects of the appearance of the control, in the Properties pane for the button. To make the button function to save the form, select the button, select "Advanced" in the Properties pane, and type "SubmitForm(Form1)" in the OnSelect field, as seen in Figure 5-12. This will submit the data as a new record to the accounts table.

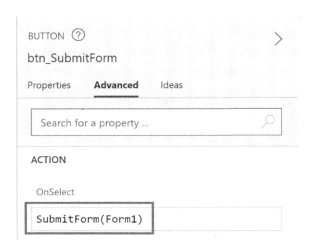

Figure 5-12. *Setting OnSelect field*

Now that you have a functional app that creates new records, simply click Save and Publish in the app actions menu.

Note   Since the app is only an interface to the data layer, any users will still need the appropriate permissions to perform data operations. Refer to Chapter 4 for guidance on how to manage the security layer to ensure your users have the appropriate permissions in place.

Components

To get started with building a component library, go to your environment, select "Apps" from the left-hand navigation bar, and select the Component Libraries tab under the Apps section. To create a new library, select "New Component Library," as seen in Figure 5-13. Give your library a name and click Create.

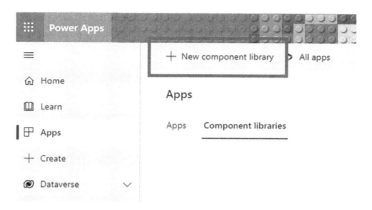

Figure 5-13. *New component library*

Building a component is like building a canvas app except each "page" is a separate component. Start by adding your controls to the screen, then customize them as necessary. Selecting the component level in the tree view on the left will display the Properties pane for the component on the right, as seen in Figure 5-14. Here you can change the default height and width of the component.

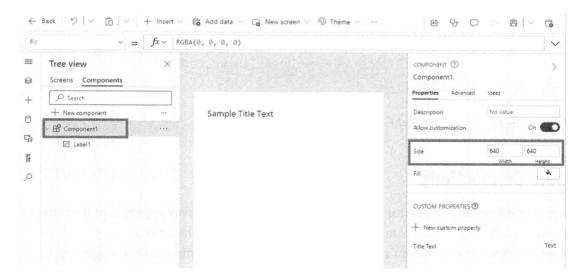

Figure 5-14. *Component properties*

This section also has the Custom Properties section, which allows you to set inputs, outputs, and actions for your component. You can think of components as functions in programming where you pass in a value, something happens, and it passes back a

145

value. The scope of the controls in a component is the component itself. So, if you want to access the values of a date picker in a component, you must set up an output property with the value of the date picker.

To set up a custom property, select "New Custom Property". to display the New Custom Property pane, as seen in Figure 5-15.

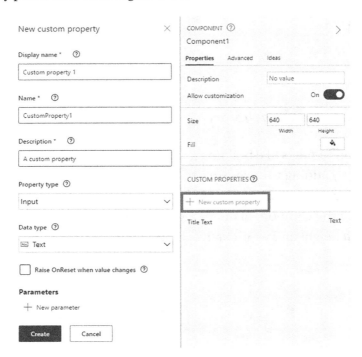

Figure 5-15. *Component Custom Property pane*

Data Connections

Another differentiating factor between model-driven and canvas apps is that the latter allow the addition of data sources other than Dataverse. Canvas apps allow you to connect to hundreds of data sources across many vendors. This allows a single app to integrate data from different systems and tie that data together in a single interface. This can simplify tasks for users as they can use a single app to accomplish tasks across multiple systems instead of having to switch between systems.

This integration is accomplished through connectors, which are essentially just wrappers built around an application programming interface (API) that allows one system to talk to another. Connectors will be covered in Chapter 6 in greater depth.

Model-Driven Apps

Model-driven apps are designed and built around Dataverse. This means that if you want to integrate with external data, the use of virtual tables in Dataverse is your best option. These apps also do not have the capability to be customized as much as canvas apps, because they are built around the Microsoft Unified Interface design. However, while model-driven apps lack flexibility, they more than make up for it in other areas.

Because model-driven apps are built specifically for Dataverse, they work very well with Dataverse. Field security profiles, covered in Chapter 4, automatically flow through to the controls in model-driven apps so a user who cannot edit a field on a record will see the control in read-only mode. Business rules, covered in Chapter 3, also pull through natively to the model-driven controls so dynamic filtering and conditional visibility of fields can be built using business rules and be applied across multiple apps and tables at once. Even business process flows (BPFs) pull into model-driven apps natively and provide a clean, simple, and functional interface.

Building a Model-Driven App

There are a few ways to build a model-driven app, but the primary method is to go into your solution and select New ➤ App ➤ Model-Driven App from the top toolbar, as seen in Figure 5-16.

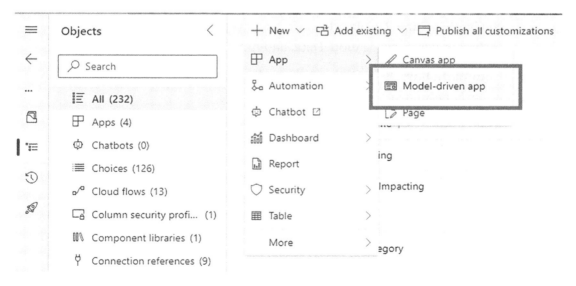

Figure 5-16. *Creating a new model-driven app*

Once your app is created, you will start adding pages, navigation, data, automation, and so forth. But, before you start doing that, it is important to become familiar with the layout of the model-driven app designer. Figure 5-17 outlines the basic sections.

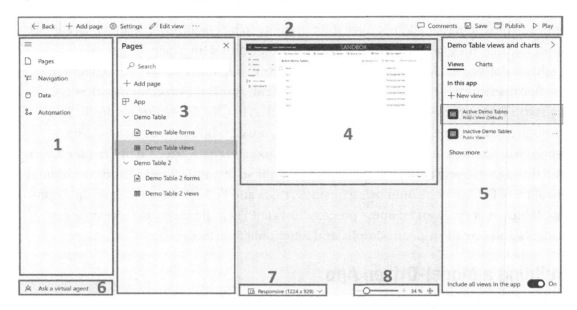

Figure 5-17. *Model-driven app designer layout*

The model-driven app designer comprises the following sections:

1. **Navigation Pane**: Displays the different layers of your app, including Pages, Navigation, Data, and Automation

2. **Command Bar**: Displays standard application commands, such as back, new page, settings, etc.

3. **Asset Pane**: Displays the assets associated with the selected layer of the app in the navigation pane

4. **App Preview**: Displays a real-time view of the app as it is configured.

5. **Property Pane**: Displays the properties of the selected component or forms and views of a selected table

6. **Virtual Agent Assistant**: A virtual chatbot to assist you with questions while building the app

7. **Preview Size Switcher**: Allows switching between different display sizes to view the app in different resolutions and devices

8. **Zoom and Fit to Screen**: Allows zooming in/out

Note   The Navigation pane collapses for a compact mode. To expand or collapse it, select the pancake menu icon at the top of the Navigation Pane, as seen in Figure 5-17.

Navigation Elements

There are layers of navigation elements in model-driven apps that help you organize your app and make it more intuitive as well as target your interface to the audience. The elements are as follows:

- **Areas**: Allow you to create entirely different workspaces in your app with a new navigation tree specific to each area

- **Groups**: Simply labels groups of multiple subareas on the left-hand navigation pane in your app. These are non-interactive design elements.

- **Subarea**: These are active navigation elements that take you to pages for tables and dashboards, as well as web pages and resources. This is how a user would navigate, for instance, from a table to a dashboard.

Note   By default, areas are disabled. If you wish to use areas in your app, select "Navigation" from the Navigation pane, select "Navigation Bar" from the Assets pane, and check the box next to "Enable Areas" in the Properties pane.

As you can see in Figure 5-18, the groups and subareas map directly to the structure shown in the app preview, but the areas are selected using a menu at the bottom of the navigation.

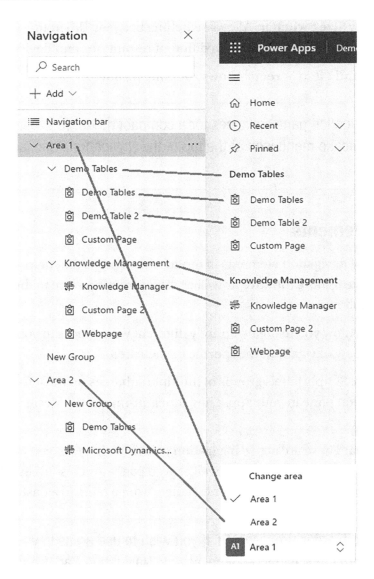

Figure 5-18. *Model-driven app navigation mapping*

Select the Navigation from the Navigation pane, and you will see that the basic navigation structure has already been built for you, as seen in Figure 5-19. This is the beginning of your navigation structure that will be displayed in your app.

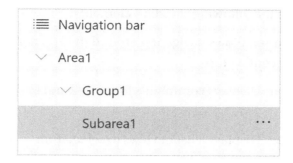

Figure 5-19. *Basic navigation structure*

Select a subarea. You will see the Properties pane displays the configuration options for that subarea. Select "Table" from the Content Type dropdown, select a table from the table dropdown, and enter a name for the section in the Title field; you will see that the app is updated with an interface for a table using the Unified Interface format, as seen in Figure 5-20.

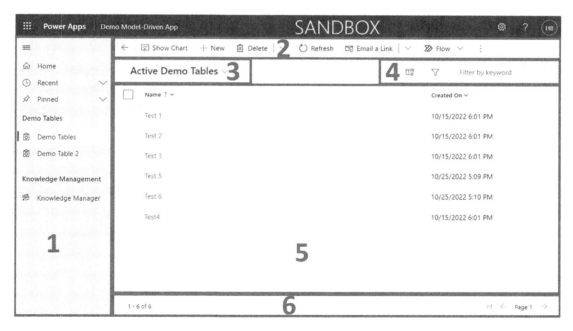

Figure 5-20. *Model-driven app Unified Interface layout*

This layout includes the following standard elements:

1. **Navigation Pane**: Allows navigation around the app and access to pinned and recent records

2. **Command Bar**: Displays commands for record and table operations

3. **View Selection**: Displays a list of views to select from

4. **Search and Column Selection**: Allows searching and filtering of records and customization of which columns are visible

5. **Record View**: Displays the specified records

6. **Pagination Navigation**: Allows navigation between the paginated records lists

As you continue to add navigation elements to the navigation list, you will see them reflected in your app, as seen in Figure 5-21, so it is important to plan this grouping out. It should be logical for users to navigate and find the information they seek.

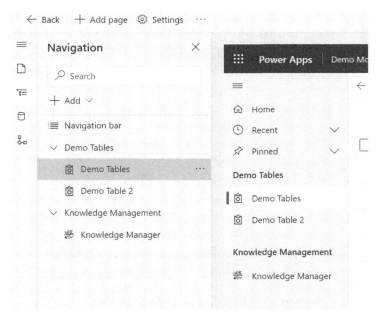

Figure 5-21. *Navigation hierarchy corresponding to app Navigation pane*

Pages

Pages are a category of subarea and include Dataverse table, dashboard, and custom pages. While the first two are self-explanatory, the third one is a bit more obscure.

Custom pages refer to canvas pages that are built specifically to integrate with model-driven apps. They provide a crossover between the two app types and allow you to leverage the layout and connector options of canvas apps, but within the context of a model-driven app. Since custom pages are a separate development effort, refer to the "Custom Pages" section in this chapter to read more about them.

Sharing Model-Driven Apps

Sharing model-driven apps is a bit more complicated than sharing a canvas app because a model-driven app requires that the member belong to a security group that has model-driven app permissions. As you can see in Figure 5-22, that setting is under the Customization tab, and the model-driven app must have Read permissions enabled.

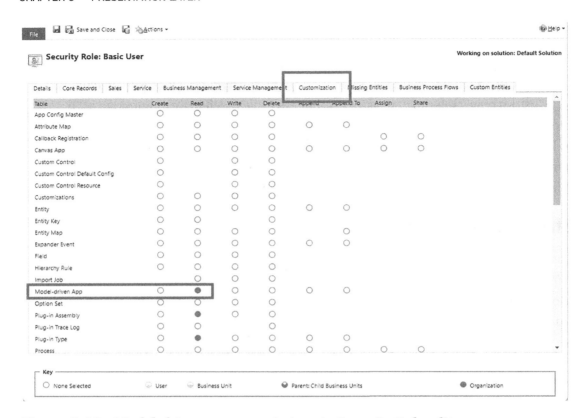

Figure 5-22. *Model-driven app permissions in Security Role editor*

Just as with other security roles, you can assign this role to a user or a team that the user is a member of to apply it.

Once the user has permission to run model-driven apps in general, you can then share the specific model-driven app with either a team or a user, just as you would share a canvas app. However, with model-driven apps, you can also share the app with a security role directly, as seen in Figure 5-23, by selecting the ellipses next to the app that you wish to share, selecting the app in the Share pane, then selecting the security role you wish to share the app with.

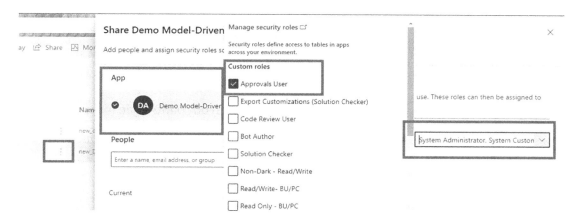

Figure 5-23. *Sharing a model-driven app with a security role*

This method allows you an additional option for security management that is not available in canvas apps and makes sense because the role dictates the access to that type of app.

Forms

Since model-driven apps are made to integrate with existing layers of the platform, you customize views and forms not in the app, but rather in the table settings. This has the advantage of your being able to configure these items in one place and utilize them across several apps. All updates to the forms and views also propagate across all apps they are used in as well, so it creates an efficient process for updating apps. In addition, the forms and views are leveraged in the native Dataverse interfaces for managing records.

Note   While views are accessible within canvas apps in the form of a query, there is no integration of native Dataverse forms in canvas apps. This means that any forms created in a canvas app need to be built in that app, or copied and pasted from another canvas app.

Form Types

There are four types of forms that can be used in model-driven apps, as follows:

- **Main**: Primary interface for interacting with records

- **Quick Create**: Allows creation of records in a flyout pane–style form

- **Quick View**: An embedded form that displays summary information of a record

- **Card**: Designed for mobile interfaces and displays data in a compact format

You can select which forms are available to your app by adding or removing them from the In This App section of the Form Properties pane. Select "Pages" in the Navigation pane, expand the table in the Assets pane, then select the table you want to operate on. Then, adjust the forms in the Properties pane, as seen in Figure 5-24.

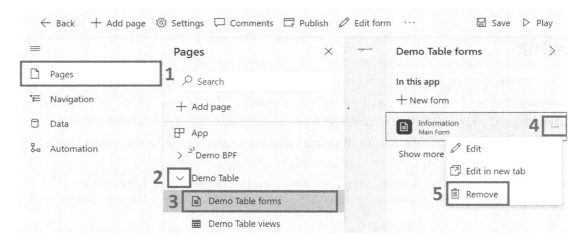

Figure 5-24. *Modifying form selection*

Editing Forms

To edit a form, you can navigate to your table settings in Dataverse and select forms to manage, as discussed in Chapter 2, or you can select "Pages" from the Navigation pane, select the table that you want to edit the views on, expand the options for your table in the Assets pane, select the forms options, then select the ellipses and edit in new tab, as seen in Figure 5-25. This will open a new window where you can edit the form.

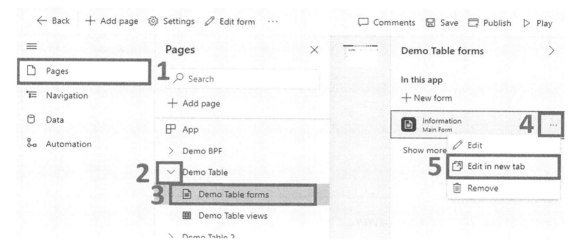

Figure 5-25. *Launching the form designer from the model-driven app designer*

The form editor makes updating forms very easy with drag-and-drop functionality and simple conditions.

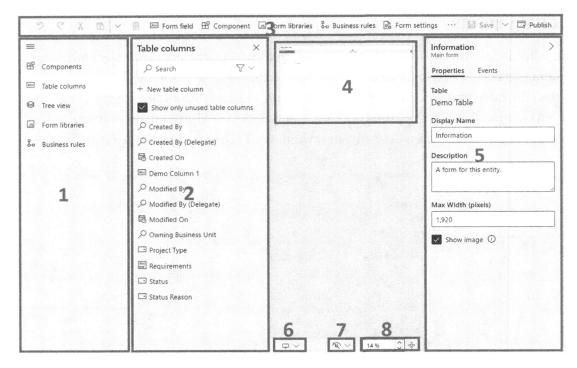

Figure 5-26. *Form editor layout*

The basic layout of the form editor can be seen in Figure 5-26 and includes the following:

1. **Navigation Pane**: Allows selecting different form element categories

2. **Asset Pane**: Displays different assets and components depending on the selection in the Navigation pane

3. **Command Bar**: Allows selection of commands such as Save and Publish, as well as navigation of different form element categories, like the Navigation pane.

4. **Form Canvas**: Displays the form as you edit it

5. **Properties Pane**: Displays properties of the selected asset or control

6. **Preview Size Switcher**: Since forms are reactive, they can appear different depending on the screen size. This allows you to test those changes.

7. **Show Hidden Controls Toggle**: Shows all hidden controls. This is off by default, but turning this on can be helpful when editing forms with conditionally hidden controls.

8. **Zoom and Fit Controls**: Allows the adjustment of the form preview zoom level

Editing Fields

To add fields to the form, simply select table columns from the Navigation pane and drag the required fields from the Asset pane to the form canvas and place it where you want the field to be. All changes to the canvas will be reflected in the tree view, regardless of whether they are visible or hidden.

Selecting a field will change the context of the Properties pane to that field so you can adjust properties such as label, visibility, and size. To build logic into your forms, you can utilize business rules, as discussed in Chapter 3, or events, which are custom JavaScript code segments. These are visible in the corresponding tabs in the Properties pane.

Certain types of fields also have alternate control types that you can use to change the look and feel of your app. For instance, some developers prefer to display a toggle instead of a dropdown, or a set of buttons instead of a multi-select combo-box dropdown control. This can be accomplished in the Components section of the Properties pane, as seen in Figure 5-27.

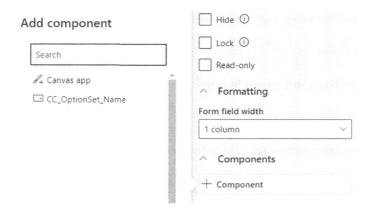

Figure 5-27. *Component settings for fields in model-driven app*

Once you select a component, you will select what interface it will be displayed for from the options Web, Mobile, and/or Tablet, as not all controls are optimal for all devices.

App Layout

Your form's layout is not simply restricted to a series of rows and columns of fields. Here is a list of some of the commonly used components in forms that help to organize data into logical groups that help users quickly find the information they are looking for:

- **Tabs**: Sort out information logically by team or phase so that forms don't become excessively long.

- **Sections**: Group data that is related, such as sponsors or dates.

- **Subgrids**: Display a related list of records, such as project team members or tasks.

- **Quick View**: Display a set of key fields from a related record, such as name, email, and department for a user record selected for the project sponsor.

- **Timeline**: Display a chronological view of related activity records, such as notes or meetings.

- **Power BI Report**: Embed Power BI reports to bring context-based reports directly into your app so users don't have to search for separate reports.

Tip   Users tend to not like excessive vertical scrolling or an excessive number of tabs, so it is important to not lean too heavily on either method; try to find a balance of the two. It also helps to keep field width and height to a minimum to make the most of the form's visible space.

To add any components, simply select them from the Navigation pane, then proceed to select or drag the components to place them on the form canvas.

When you are done working on your form, click Save and Publish; the form will automatically be updated anywhere that form is used.

Custom Pages

Custom pages allow a crossover between model-driven and canvas apps so that the design elements and data sources from canvas apps can be incorporated into model-driven apps. Custom pages run in the model-driven app as a subsection, like a table or a dashboard, so it is easy for a user to switch between the contexts in the single navigation bar of the model-driven app.

Creating a Custom Page

From your solution, select New ➤ App ➤ Page, as seen in Figure 5-28.

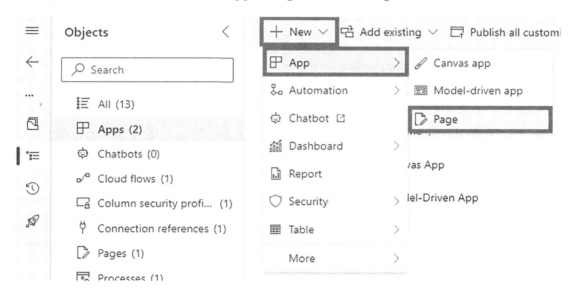

Figure 5-28. *Creating a new custom page in a solution*

As you can see in Figure 5-29, the custom page uses the Power Apps Studio discussed in the "Canvas Apps" section of this chapter. However, there are additional options in the development canvas area that are specific to pages. There are also no options to add pages, as a custom page is limited to a single page.

Figure 5-29. *Custom pages designer*

Tip   Refer to this section to become familiar with the Power Apps Studio if you are not already.

One of the neat features available in this section is that you can select the With Data template and select a table, and the pages designer will create a standard interface based on that table. From there you can continue to customize the page as you would any other canvas app, then save and publish.

Add Custom Page to Model-Driven App

To add a custom page to a model-driven app, simply select "Add Page" and then select "Custom Page" from the options, as seen in Figure 5-30.

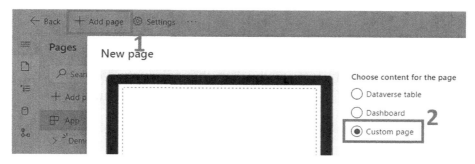

Figure 5-30. *Adding a custom page to model-driven app*

The next screen will give you the option to either create a new page or use an existing one, as seen in Figure 5-31.

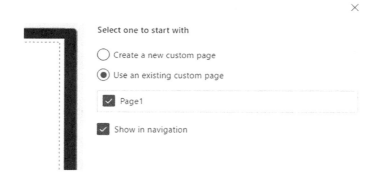

Figure 5-31. *Options when adding custom page to model-driven app*

Select "Add" and the page will be added to your app.

Note   As you can see in Figure 5-31, you can create a new page from the app as well, but I typically lean toward creating new assets in the Solution pane to be consistent.

Reports

While apps are primarily meant to edit data, reports are meant to access data. Because reports are targeted at simply accessing the data, they will contain visualizations that focus more on telling a story and interpreting data than a form in an app would.

Dataverse Reports

The native Dataverse reports allow some basic reporting capabilities, primarily focused around displaying data in a list or hierarchy view, as seen in Figure 5-32.

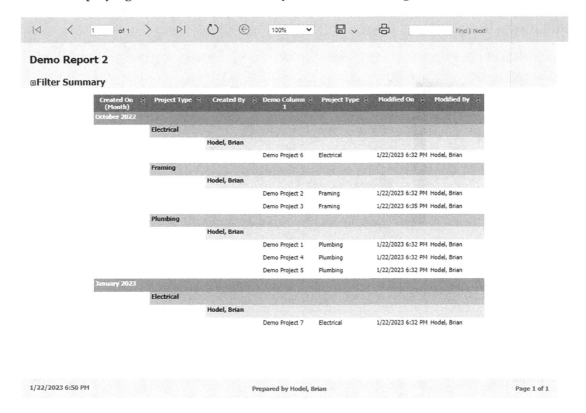

Figure 5-32. *Example of Dataverse report*

To create a new Dataverse report, navigate to your solution and select New ➤ Report. A new window will open with the report builder, as seen in Figure 5-33.

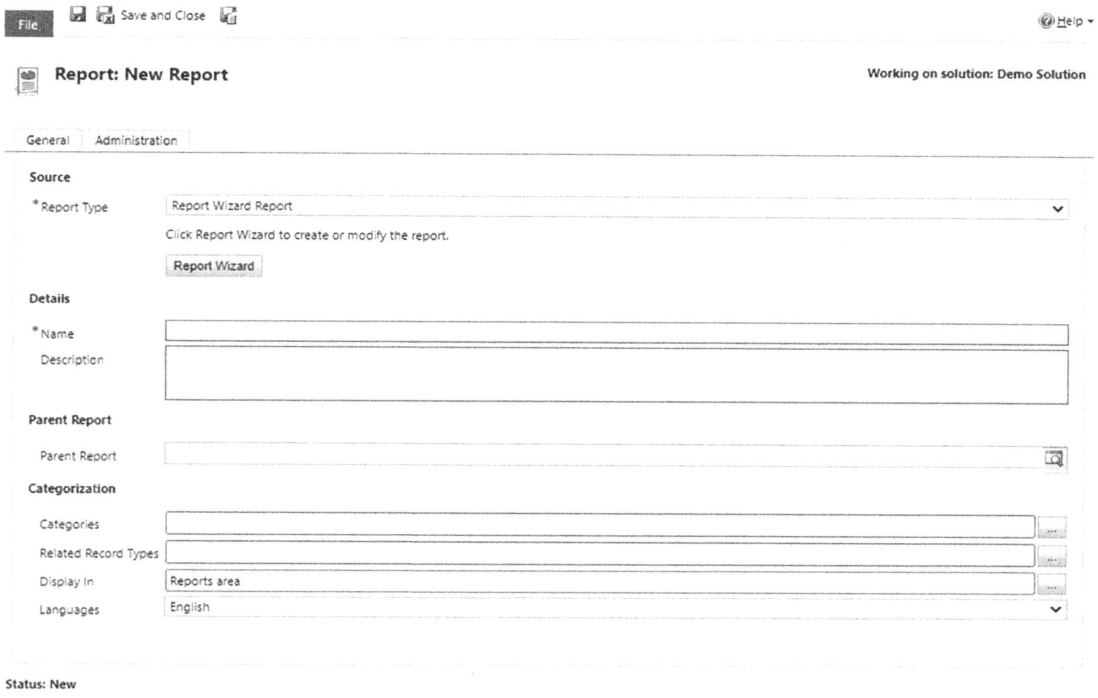

File   Save and Close   Help ▾

Report: New Report   Working on solution: Demo Solution

General   Administration

Source

* Report Type   Report Wizard Report   ⌄

Click Report Wizard to create or modify the report.

Report Wizard

Details

* Name

Description

Parent Report

Parent Report   🔍

Categorization

Categories   ...

Related Record Types   ...

Display In   Reports area   ...

Languages   English   ⌄

Status: New

Figure 5-33. *Report builder*

In the Source section, select "Run Report Wizard" from the Report Type dropdown. The other options in this list are for if you have an existing report file that you want to import or a web page that you want to point to.

Next, click the Report Wizard button to start building your report. A new window will open, as seen in Figure 5-34. The first screen allows you to select "Start a new report" or "Start from an existing report," as seen in Figure 5-34. Often, you can start with existing reports and modify them for your needs. However, for this case, we will create a new report, so select "Start a new report" and click Next.

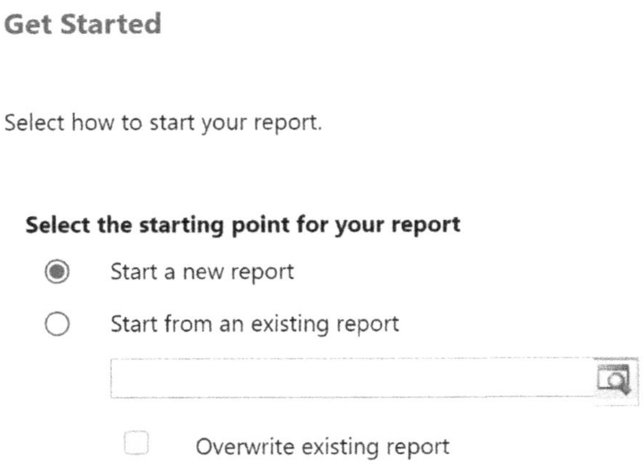

Get Started

Select how to start your report.

Select the starting point for your report

◉   Start a new report

○   Start from an existing report

[🔍]

☐   Overwrite existing report

Figure 5-34. *Get Started wizard*

Once you get to the Report Properties window, you will see several options to begin your report, as seen in Figure 5-35.

- **Report Name**: Give your report a name that will describe what it does. This name should be short and specific as it will show up in the list of reports in the model-driven app.

- **Report Description**: Allow users to see details of the purpose of the report.

- **Primary Record Type**: The primary table that your report will be based on

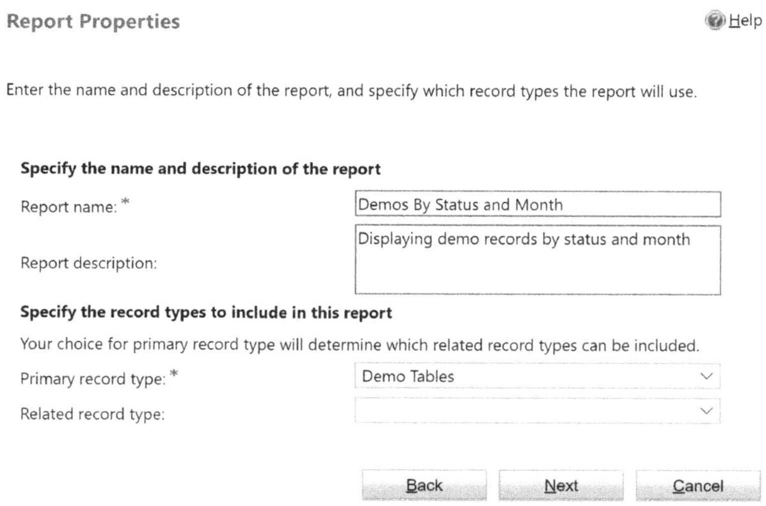

Report Properties   ⑦ Help

Enter the name and description of the report, and specify which record types the report will use.

Specify the name and description of the report

Report name: * | Demos By Status and Month |

Report description: | Displaying demo records by status and month |

Specify the record types to include in this report

Your choice for primary record type will determine which related record types can be included.

Primary record type: * | Demo Tables   ∨ |

Related record type: | ∨ |

[Back]   [Next]   [Cancel]

Figure 5-35. *Setting report properties*

Click Next to move to the "Select Record to Include in Report" screen.

If you have an existing view that you want to use to filter the records on your report, you can select it in the Use Saved View dropdown. Otherwise, select "[new]" and enter your filter criteria, as seen in Figure 5-36.

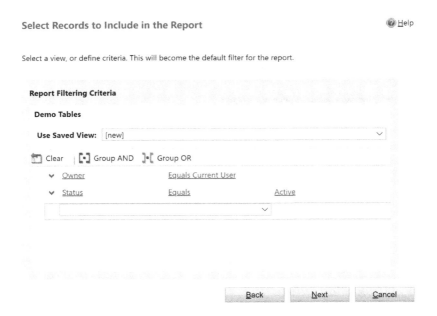

Figure 5-36. *Creating report filter criteria in report wizard*

As you can see in Figure 5-36, this filter will return only records where the User field is equal to the current logged-in user and the status of the record is Active.

Note   Since Status is an Option Set value, you will select the ellipses next to the field value to select the appropriate option, since an Option Set cannot be queried based on a text value.

You can use And / Or group logic by selecting the "Group AND" or "Group OR" buttons to create more complex query logic.

Once you are done setting up your query parameters, click the Next button to move to the Lay Out Fields screen, as seen in Figure 5-37.

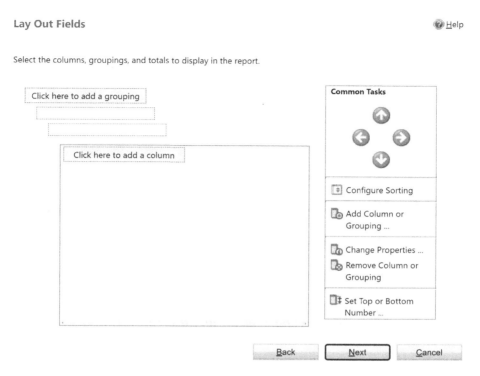

Figure 5-37. *Lay Out Fields screen in report wizard*

In this window, there are three primary sections, as follows:

- **1 – Grouping**: Allows you to configure the hierarchy of grouping records in your view.

- **2 – Columns**: Allows you to define the data that is displayed for each row.

- **3 – Controls**: Allows you to move fields around using cursor, as well as configure sorting and other settings for the fields.

Selecting "Click here to add a grouping" opens a new dialogue to select a field for the selected level, as well as properties of that field, as seen in Figure 5-38.

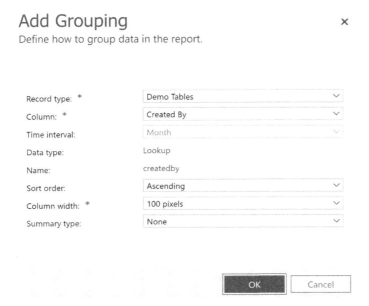

Figure 5-38. *Add Grouping screen in report wizard*

Selecting "Click here to add a column" will bring up a similar dialogue to select the field that will show up in the record row.

Tip   Since the grouping contains information about the record, you usually do not need to add those same columns to the record since it is duplicative.

Once you have finished configuring the settings for your report layout, click Next to move to the Format Report window, as seen in Figure 5-39.

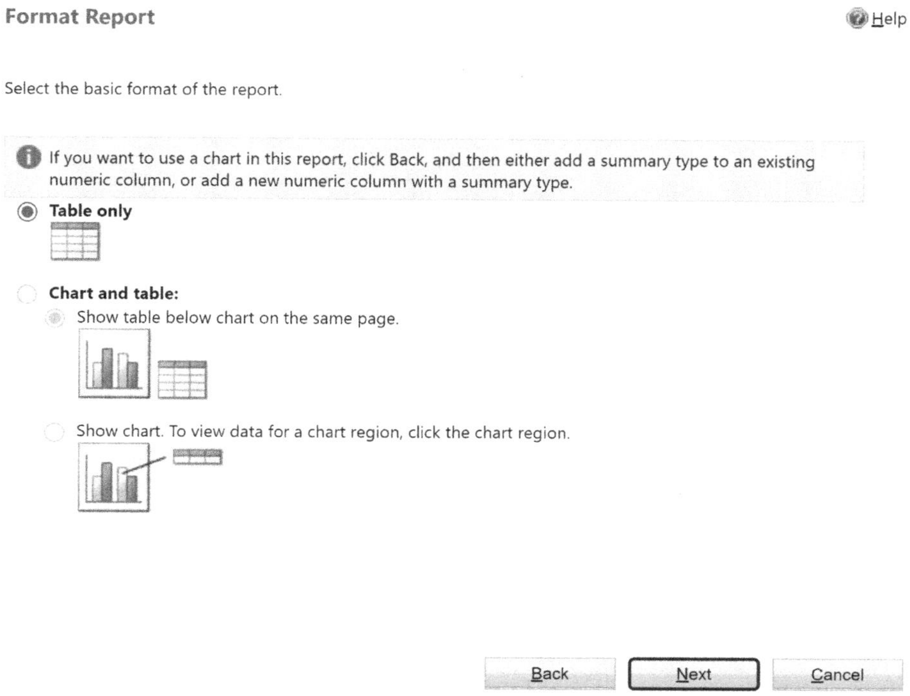

Format Report   ⓘ Help

Select the basic format of the report.

> ⓘ If you want to use a chart in this report, click Back, and then either add a summary type to an existing
> numeric column, or add a new numeric column with a summary type.

◉ **Table only**

○ **Chart and table:**

    ◉ Show table below chart on the same page.

    ○ Show chart. To view data for a chart region, click the chart region.

Back   Next   Cancel

Figure 5-39. *Format Report window*

The basic report will have Table Only selected. However, if you have summary columns set up in the Lay Out Fields screen, you can select the option to add a chart to your report.

Click the Next button to view the report summary, then click the Finish button to close the wizard. You will notice that the fields on the Report Builder screen are now filled out. Simply click the Save and Close button and your report is done.

Once your report is saved, it will show up in your model-driven apps when the appropriate table is selected, as seen in Figure 5-40.

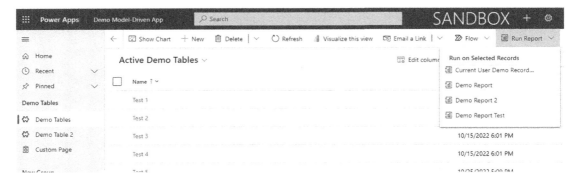

Figure 5-40. *Report list in model-driven app*

Now, users can run formatted reports right from the context of the tables they are looking at in the model-driven app, which can reduce the number of tools that they need to manage.

Power BI Reports

As I said before, Dataverse reports are fairly limited in the amount of customization that can be done to them. If you have more complex reporting requirements, Power BI can be integrated into your solutions and apps as well.

While how to use Power BI is beyond this book's scope, adding Power BI reports to Dataverse is simple.

Navigate to your solution, select Add Existing ➤ Analytics ➤ Power BI Report, as seen in Figure 5-41.

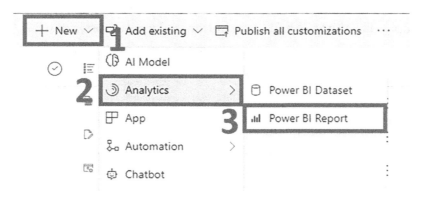

Figure 5-41. *Add Power BI report to solution*

After adding your report to the solution, you can add the associated Power BI dashboards from your solution as well by navigating to your solution and selecting New ➤ Dashboard ➤ Power BI Embedded, as seen in Figure 5-42.

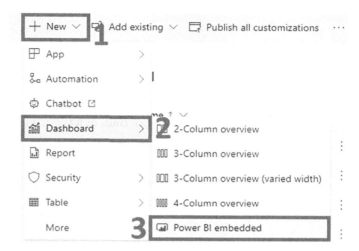

Figure 5-42. *Adding a Power BI embedded report to solution*

A dialogue will open where you can select a Power BI report or Power BI dashboard to add to your solution, as seen in Figure 5-43.

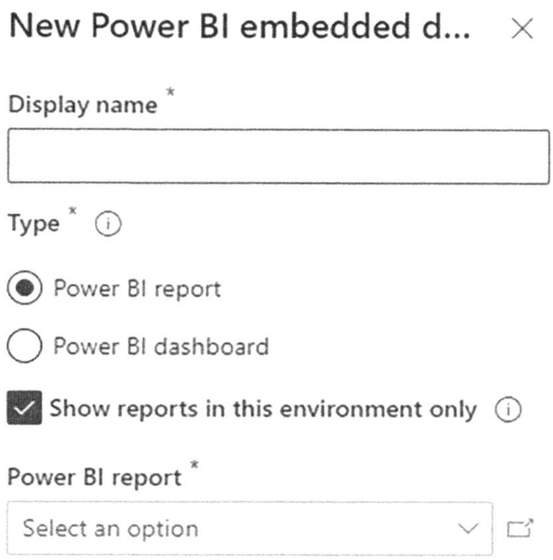

New Power BI embedded d...   ✕

Display name *

Type * ⓘ

◉ Power BI report

◯ Power BI dashboard

☑ Show reports in this environment only ⓘ

Power BI report *

Select an option   ⌄   ⌐

Figure 5-43. *Selecting Power BI asset to add to Solution*

After you add these assets from Power BI, you can add them to your apps the same way you add other dashboards to your app.

This allows you to build far more complex reports and dashboards to add to your apps.

Summary

In summary, the presentation layer allows users to interact with data in meaningful and intuitive ways. Apps allow the reading and editing of data at a record level, and reports and dashboards allow analysis of the data. Both are important in the scope of business, and the more you can merge the two methods, the better the experience your users will likely have. Next, you will learn how to integrate data from other systems to allow your systems to work together and reduce or eliminate data discrepancies.

CHAPTER 6

Integration with Third-Party Tools

In the previous chapter, we discussed the Presentation Layer and how to make your data useful to end users using apps and reports. In this chapter, we will discuss the ability to integrate your solutions with third-party data to create seamlessly integrated processes to simplify work across teams and tools. Through the use of Connectors, Dataflows, and Virtual Tables, you can adapt or extend legacy tools easier than ever before. These features help you to be agile as your business changes, but do not require teams to move off of tools that work for what they do now.

Connectors

Connectors are essentially wrappers built around an application programming interface (API) that allow one system to talk to another. Connectors consist of two components: actions and triggers.

Actions: Requests to perform operations on data, such as create, read, write, and delete.

Triggers: Provide a notification that an event has occurred. There are two types of triggers: push and polling. Push triggers listen to an endpoint until an action has occurred, such as a file being uploaded or a record being updated. Polling triggers run on a schedule, such as every day at 1 AM.

Connectors are available for use in Power Apps, Power Automate, and Azure Logic Apps, the availability of actions and triggers may differ depending on which product you are using.

It is also important to be familiar with the various categories of connectors available in Power Platform and understand where each one stands with regard to source, ownership, and licensing.

© Brian Hodel 2023
B. Hodel, *Beginning Microsoft Dataverse*, https://doi.org/10.1007/978-1-4842-9334-8_6

Out-of-the-Box Connectors

Microsoft provides an extensive list of connectors certified for use in Power Platform.

Microsoft Published

Microsoft-published connectors are created and published by Microsoft. This includes connectors for many Microsoft systems as well as many non-Microsoft systems. This differs from Verified Publisher connectors that are created by a third party and verified by Microsoft.

Verified Publisher

Verified-publisher connectors are connectors that were built by third parties that own the underlying service they are integrating with. There is an extensive review process involving testing by both Microsoft and Microsoft partners before a verified-publisher connector is published to the platform. After that initial review, any updates are also subject to a review process. This is to ensure that any verified-publisher connectors are stable and reliable to be used in production systems.

Independent Publisher

Independent-publisher connectors are a new concept on the platform and allow third parties who do NOT own the underlying service to develop new connectors. This adds a new stream of development that has increased the availability of integration tools between Power Platform and other services. It is also a fantastic way to contribute to the community. If you have a need to integrate with another system, it is highly likely that others do as well. So, if you are going to build a new connector, you might as well share it on the platform.

Custom Connectors

While the Power Platform has hundreds of connectors available Out-of-the-Box (OOB), it also provides the ability to create Custom Connectors to extend those capabilities. While you can make API calls from Power Automate flows using the HTTP actions, you cannot make them directly from apps unless you create a custom connector or invoke a flow. In addition, API calls made from within flows need to be configured individually and can be time-consuming. Custom connectors allow you to create a single place where the code and authentication are managed. Once you have done that, you simply add that connector to your apps and flows and ask it to perform the operations you need, just like any other connector.

The easiest way to create a custom connector is to create one from an existing Postman collection or an OpenAPI definition. These are two standard API definition formats that can be downloaded from many service providers' websites if you search through the developer resources section or by searching in Postman for existing collections of API calls.

Once you have the API definition file downloaded, navigate to your Power Platform environment, expand the Data section on the left-hand navigation bar, and select "Custom Connectors," as seen in Figure 6-1.

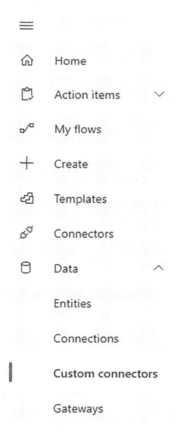

Figure 6-1. Access custom connector page

Here you will see all the custom connectors, if there are any, and can create new ones by selecting one of the options in the list, as seen in Figure 6-2.

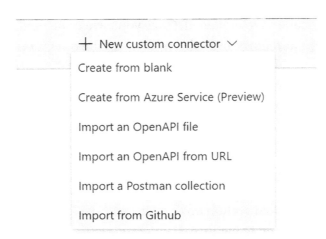

***Figure 6-2.** Creating new custom connector options*

As you can see, there are many ways to begin creating a connector, but importing an existing definition is the easiest method. In this example, I will show the process of importing an existing Postman collection, as it is one of the most common methods. Postman is a great tool for building, editing, and testing APIs. If you haven't used it before, I highly recommend you download it and begin learning how to use it (`https://www.postman.com/`).

After selecting "Import a Postman collection" you will be asked for the name of the connector and to import the Postman collection that you will have previously downloaded. Then, click Continue and the collection will be imported to your connector and generate the structure for your connector.

Once the custom connector page opens, you will see there are five tabs dedicated to configuring the connector, as follows:

- **General**: Description and base API settings, as well as option to connect over an on-premises data gateway.

- **Security**: Authentication settings for your connector. Select from No Authentication, Basic Authentication, API Key, or OAuth 2.0.

- **Definition**: Contains the API call definitions that will allow you to request and post data.

- **Code (Preview)**: Allows running of code along with the API call.

- **Test**: Allows testing of API calls prior to adding the connector to your flows and apps.

Note   Preview items are marked as "Not for use in production" by Microsoft as they are subject to change or removal.

The General tab contains the base configuration for the connector and needs to be filled out if it was not already populated during import, as seen in Figure 6-3. The elements are as follows:

- **Icon and Description**: Load an icon, color, and description for the connector to help identify it to users.

- **Connect via On-Premises Data Gateway**: Allow connecting via a gateway. This is useful if you need to connect to systems that are behind a firewall.

- **Scheme, Host, and Base URL**: Root connection parameters for the API calls.

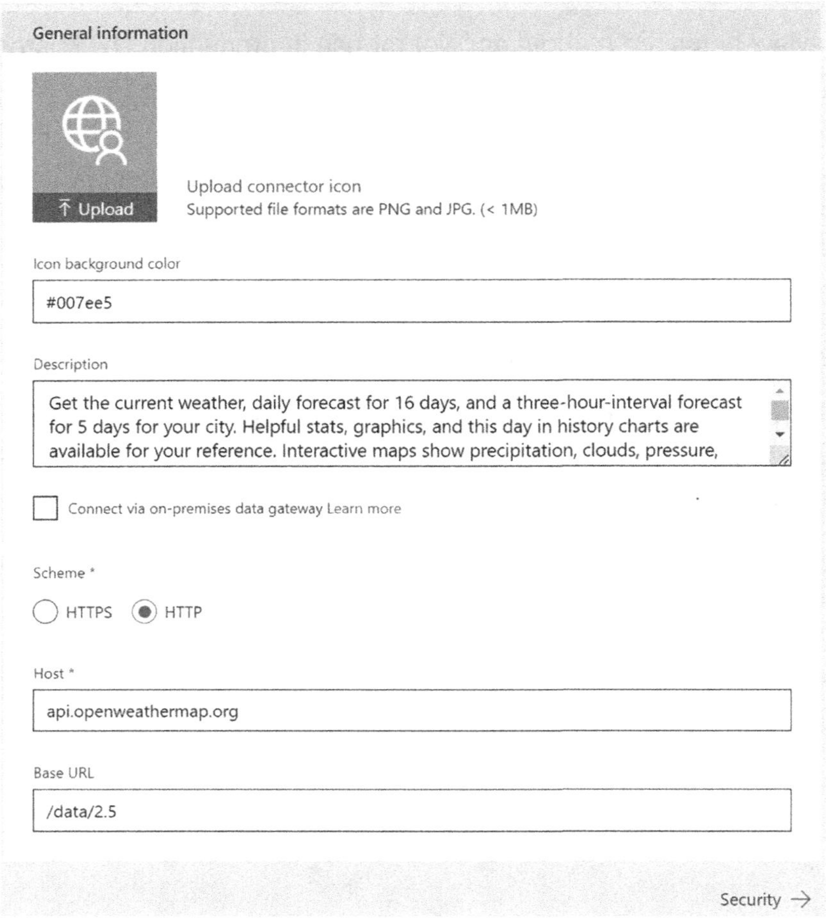

General information

↑ Upload

Upload connector icon
Supported file formats are PNG and JPG. (< 1MB)

Icon background color

#007ee5

Description

Get the current weather, daily forecast for 16 days, and a three-hour-interval forecast for 5 days for your city. Helpful stats, graphics, and this day in history charts are available for your reference. Interactive maps show precipitation, clouds, pressure,

☐ Connect via on-premises data gateway Learn more

Scheme *

◯ HTTPS   ⦿ HTTP

Host *

api.openweathermap.org

Base URL

/data/2.5

Security →

Figure 6-3. *General tab of customer connector configuration*

The Security tab contains multiple authentication methods and may need some additional details if the API call requires authentication. In this example, we are using an API Key authentication, so we will specify the parameter name and location for the parameter, as well as provide a friendly label for users when they are prompted for the API Key while setting up the connection, as seen in Figure 6-4.

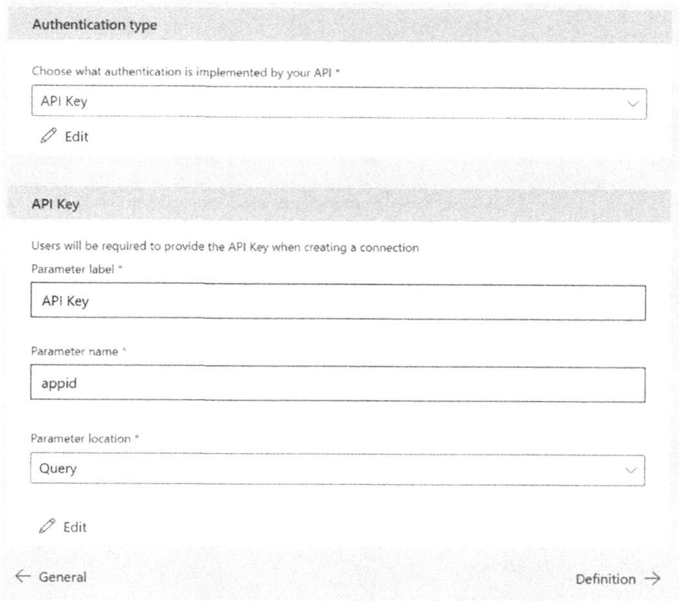

Authentication type

Choose what authentication is implemented by your API *

API Key

✎ Edit

API Key

Users will be required to provide the API Key when creating a connection

Parameter label *

API Key

Parameter name *

appid

Parameter location *

Query

✎ Edit

← General   Definition →

Figure 6-4. *Security tab of customer connector configuration*

Next is the Definition tab, as seen in Figure 6-5. This section has all the API definitions and details for the actual requests. The Actions section lists all the API calls that are defined, and the General and Request sections show the details for each request. Since we started from a Postman file, you should not need to modify this section, but it is good to understand what is going on here and customize the calls if you want to by adding or removing elements as you see fit.

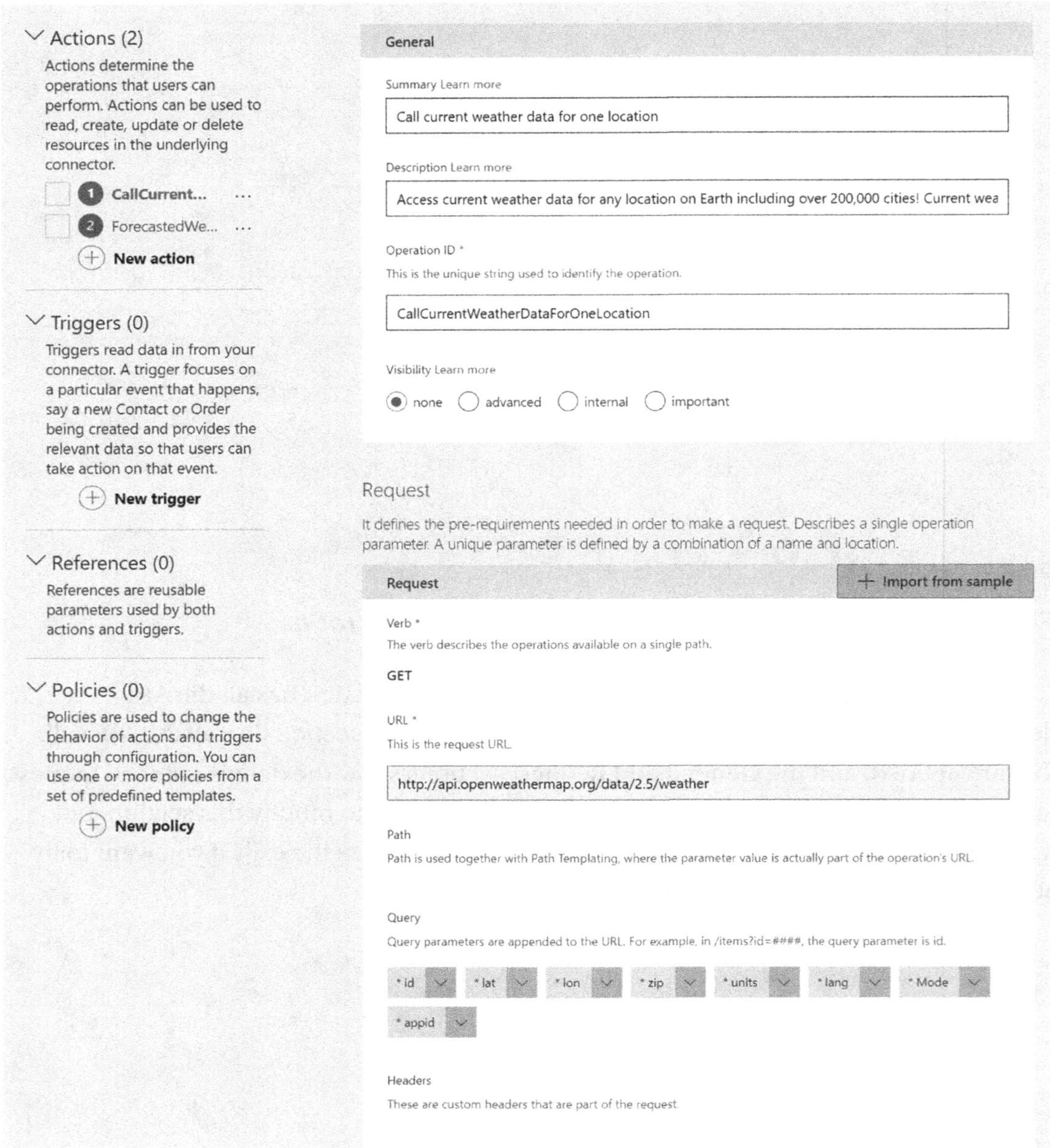

Figure 6-5. *Definition tab of customer connector configuration*

The Code tab is specifically for advanced operations that require running code at the time of the calls. We will skip this section because of the scope of this book, but it is available if needed.

When you select the Test tab, you will see a message stating that you need to create the connector before testing, which is saving and provisioning your connector. To do this, select "Create Connector" from the top command bar, as seen in Figure 6-6.

Figure 6-6. *Creating connector in custom connector configuration*

After creating your connector, you will notice that the Test Operation button is grayed out and the Selected Connection field says "None," as seen in Figure 6-7. To test your connector, you will need to create a connection to provide the authentication information. To do this, select "+ New Connection," as seen in Figure 6-7.

Figure 6-7. *Creating a connection for custom connector testing*

Since our authentication method was API Key, we are prompted to enter the API Key, as seen in Figure 6-8. Once your connection is set up, you can begin testing your API to ensure everything is working as expected.

Figure 6-8. *Entering API Key while creating connection*

Note   If the Test Operation button is still greyed out after creating your connection, you may need to select the refresh icon in the upper-right corner of the Connections box to refresh the interface.

The Test section contains the connection configuration and testing capabilities for your API calls, as seen in Figure 6-9. Test API calls by entering values in the parameter fields and clicking the Test Operation button. Your request will be sent to the service, and a response will be returned to the Response section.

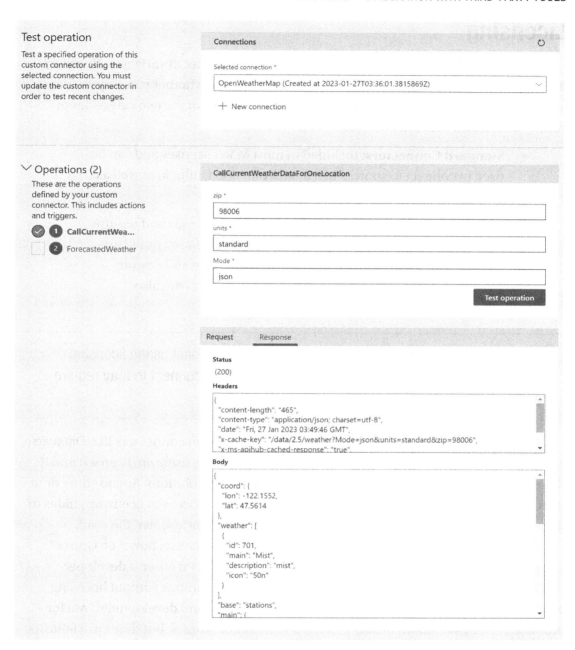

Figure 6-9. *Test connector functions screen*

Once your testing is complete, you can start using your connector to integrate data from other systems into your solution.

Licensing

Licensing across Power Platform is complex and involves a lot of variables. However, the class of connector used in your app or flow will dictate whether you may need an additional license for your app or flow. Here is an overview of the two categories of connectors to be aware of:

- **Standard Connectors**: Included in most M365 licenses and can be used to connect to sources like SharePoint and Outlook, as well as many other non-Microsoft systems.

- **Premium Connectors**: Not included in M365 licenses and require additional licenses, such as per app or per user. These connectors are indicated by a diamond icon in lists. Dataverse and custom connectors are in this category. Custom connectors are also considered Premium and require a license.

Note   While Microsoft generally does not require additional usage licensing on standard connectors, some of the services that they connect to may require licensing to use them.

The licensing for Power Platform, especially for Premium connectors like Dataverse, can get complicated. It is important to understand how your users are licensed and if there may be additional costs to deploying your Dataverse solutions. Spend some time with the organization's licensing teams and reviewing the Microsoft licensing guides to ensure that you don't run into unexpected licensing roadblocks down the road.

There are a couple of loopholes in the licensing for Dataverse, however. One is Dataverse for Teams, which is discussed later in this book. The other is developer environments, which allow developers to build and test solutions without licensing considerations. These environments are meant for testing and development, not for production, and are automatically deleted if inactive for 90 days, but they are a fantastic way to get in and build solutions on Dataverse without having to worry about licensing barriers.

Note   Developer environments should not be used as part of an ALM process. For any ALM-type development process, Sandbox environments should be set up and used.

Virtual Tables

Virtual tables enable you to work with external data sources within Dataverse without the need to duplicate the data in Dataverse tables. Virtual tables give you a view of the data in your external data sources and allow you to relate data to data in other Dataverse tables and even to update data in the external source without having to build any sync operations.

While connectors allow you to integrate with data using the same systems as virtual tables do, such as SQL and SharePoint, virtual tables allow you to interact with that data just like you would any other table in Dataverse. Not only can you perform full Create, Read, Update, and Delete (CRUD) functions on the data, but you can also relate the data in a virtual table to other Dataverse tables, such as creating lookup fields to those tables. This allows for more seamless data integration with regards to architecture.

To create a new Virtual Table, select New Table ➤ New Table from External Data from within your solution, as seen in Figure 6-10.

Figure 6-10.   *Create new table from external data*

If you do not already have a connection, you will need to click New Connection, which will open a new browser tab/window where you can create a new connection, as seen in Figure 6-11.

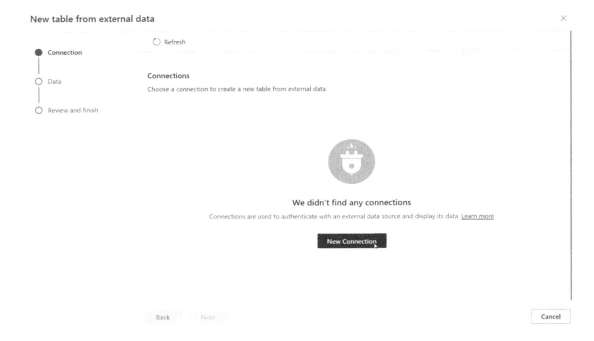

Figure 6-11. *Create a new connection for an external data source.*

If you were to connect to a SharePoint Online list, you would select SharePoint, Connect directly, then click Create, as is seen in Figure 6-12.

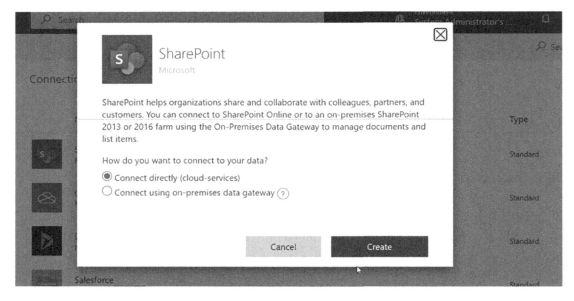

Figure 6-12. *Creating a new connection to SharePoint Online*

After you authenticate the connection, it will be created. Switch back to the New Table from External Data tab and click Refresh; your new data source will show up as shown in Figure 6-13.

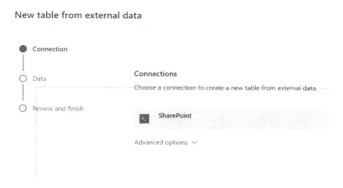

Figure 6-13.   *Connection listed in New Table from External Data window*

Click Next, and you will be able to name the connection reference, as seen in Figure 6-14. You will be able to give a friendly display name, and the Logical Name field will be automatically populated. There is no need to change the logical name from the default value.

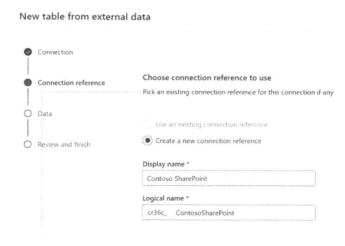

Figure 6-14.   *Naming the connection reference*

After clicking Next, you will enter the SharePoint site URL or select from the list of recent sites if available. Click Next again and select the list to which you want to connect, as seen in Figure 6-15.

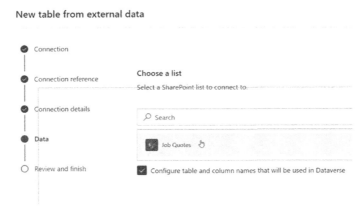

Figure 6-15. *Selecting list from virtual table setup screen*

Next, you can set the display name of the table and select the primary field from the list of fields that exist in the SharePoint list, as seen in Figure 6-16. The grayed-out properties cannot be changed and are used by Dataverse with default values.

Figure 6-16. *Selecting primary field in virtual table setup*

After clicking Create, you will be shown both the SharePoint list details and the new Dataverse virtual table details side-by-side. Click Finish to complete the operation.

Once the creation operation is finished, you can navigate to the table and view the table columns and data like looking at a normal Dataverse table.

You can now create lookup columns in other Dataverse tables that connect to the new virtual table just like any other table. In this manner, you can relate records from your SharePoint list source to Dataverse tables in the same way you do with other tables without ever having to duplicate your SharePoint list data in Dataverse.

You can also edit the data in your virtual table, which will automatically update the data in your SharePoint list because you are operating on the SharePoint data directly, not on Dataverse data. This seamless integration opens a great number of capabilities in system integration.

Dataverse for Teams

Dataverse for Teams (DfT) is a version of Dataverse meant for use inside Teams. One of the advantages of DfT is that you can utilize the Dataverse storage and features without additional licensing, as the DfT is included in M365 licensing models. There are limitations to consider when deciding to use DfT, such as the following:

- 2 GB storage limit per DfT environment

- 1 DfT environment per team

- DfT apps cannot be used outside of Teams without a license.

- Premium connectors aside from Dataverse still have licensing restrictions.

A safe way to look at DfT is that it allows you to build and use tools for a team but is not intended for enterprise-level tools. However, if you were to build a set of tools in a DfT environment and needed to extend them, there is a process to upgrade your DfT environment to a full environment. This is a great feature that prevents you from needing to rebuild or migrate your tools into Dataverse if they scale beyond the limitation of DfT.

Get Started

To start using Dataverse for Teams, from within Teams, open the App Store, find Power Apps, and click Add. This will add the Power Apps app to your Teams so you can start building DfT.

Use Power Apps in Teams by selecting the ellipses on the left-hand navigation bar to open the More Apps section, then search for "Power Apps," as seen in Figure 6-17.

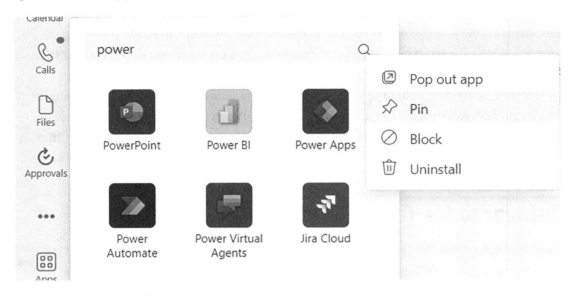

Figure 6-17. *Adding or pinning Power Apps app in Teams*

Tip   You can pin the Power Apps app to your left-hand navigation bar by selecting the ellipses on Power Apps and selecting Pin, as seen in Figure 6-17.

If you are ready to start building a new canvas apps, you can click Start Now on the Home screen to select an environment and start building a new app in the DfT Power Apps Studio or select "Learn More" to be taken to some resources to learn how to build canvas apps, as seen in Figure 6-18.

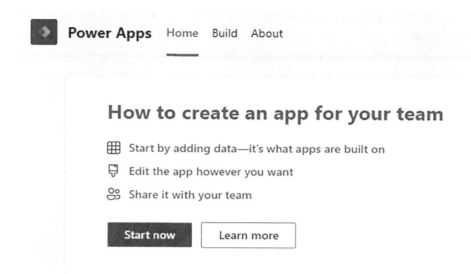

Figure 6-18. *Getting started in Dataverse for Teams*

Further down the Home page are recently accessed apps, links to DfT templates available for download from GitHub, and additional learning resource links. The templates are fully functional solutions and can be downloaded and installed to your DfT environment or even published to your tenant for others to install. These are great ways to get going in DfT, but can also be customized or expanded as you see fit using the Power Apps app in Teams. Modifying the template apps is also an effective way to learn how to build apps in DfT. I suggest you set up a "playground" team to do this in just in case you break something while learning.

Navigating the Interface

Selecting "Build" on the top navigation bar takes you to what is the equivalent of the environments list for Dataverse. This list will show only Teams environments that already have a DfT instance associated with them. Since DfT instances are only created on-demand, creating an new app for a team will automatically provision the DfT instance and appear in this list.

Note   Since DfT environments are not listed in the Power Platform interfaces, you must access any DfT resources through the Teams Power Apps app.

To create a new app for a team, select Create from the bottom of the Build screen, as seen in Figure 6-9.

This view shows a list of each DfT environment you are a member of and a list of assets in the selected DfT environment, as seen in Figure 6-19. It also shows any installed apps or dataflows that exist in the selected environment.

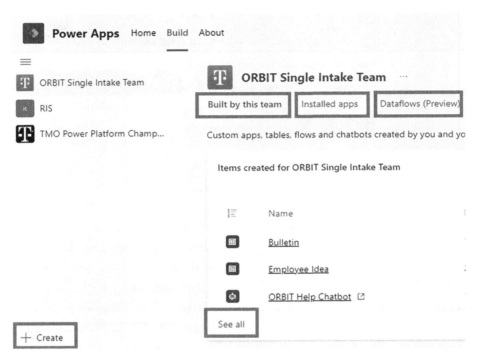

Figure 6-19. *Build section of DfT interface*

To create a new app for a team, select Create from the bottom of the Build screen, as seen in Figure 6-9. To see all of the existing apps, flows, tables, etc., or create new ones, for an existing DfT environment, select "See All", as seen in Figure 6-20. This is typically the view that I work in as it allows full control over asset creation.

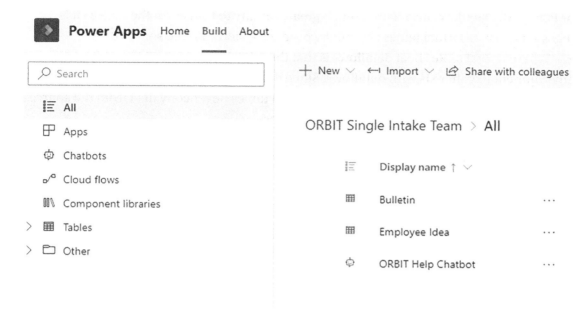

Figure 6-20. *Power Apps for Teams build items list*

If you do not see your environment listed, it could be because you have not created a DfT environment for your team yet. DfT environments are only created when an asset is added to it, so simply select "Create" at the bottom of the screen to start your environment creation. Select your environment from the list and add an app to it.

Dataflows

Dataflows are not unique to Dataverse. In fact, they exist throughout Power Platform. Their purpose is to take data from one system, manipulate it using Power Query, and bring it into the Microsoft ecosystem; in the case of Dataverse, to move it into a Dataverse table.

Dataflows vs. Virtual Tables

Dataflows can achieve some of the same functionality as virtual tables in that they can ingest data from other sources and place that data into a Dataverse table, but dataflows can also place that data in a variety of other storage locations, such as Azure Synapse or Power BI. Dataflows also have a much greater ability to transform the data as it is ingested whereas virtual tables essentially produce a view into the source data.

Where virtual tables beat dataflows is that there is no duplication of data in your environment like there is with dataflows. Since dataflows copy data from the source to destination, there is a duplication of data. Virtual tables never copy data from the source and instead query on demand to return the values.

Creating a Dataflow

To create a dataflow to Dataverse, select "Dataflows" from under Dataverse in the left-hand navigation bar in Power Apps, as seen in Figure 6-21.

Figure 6-21. *Adding a new dataflow in Power Apps*

Once the dataflows interface opens, select "New Dataflow" from the top navigation bar then "Start From Blank."

A dialogue will open, and you will give the dataflow a name. Select whether it is an analytical entity. Analytical entities are loaded to the data lake instead of Dataverse because they are meant for analysis. In this case, do not select "Analytical Entities Only."

Click the Create button.

A new window will open listing all the data sources available, as seen in Figure 6-22. Depending on what source you select, your next steps will be different, but the guide walks you through the setup.

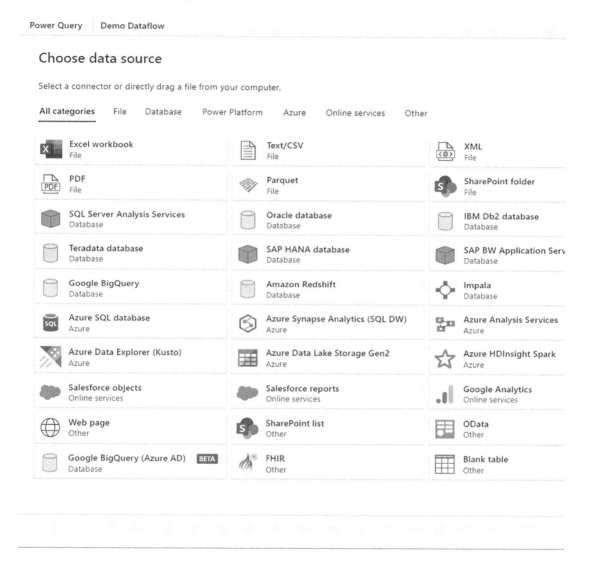

Figure 6-22. *List of dataflow connection options*

Selecting "Excel" will open a new dialogue to select your document and create a connection to Excel if one does not exist already, as seen in Figure 6-23.

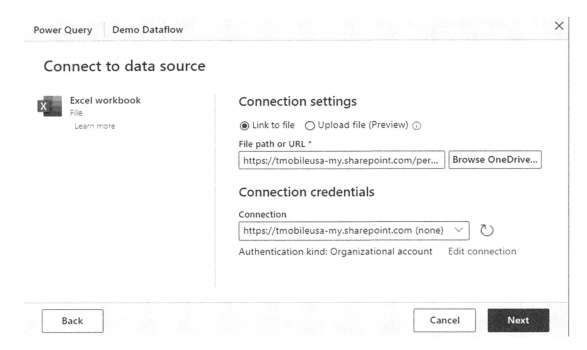

Figure 6-23. *Configuring Excel document connection*

After clicking Next, you will see a list of the sheets found in the Excel document, as seen in Figure 6-24. Select the sheet with the data you want to import and click Transform Data.

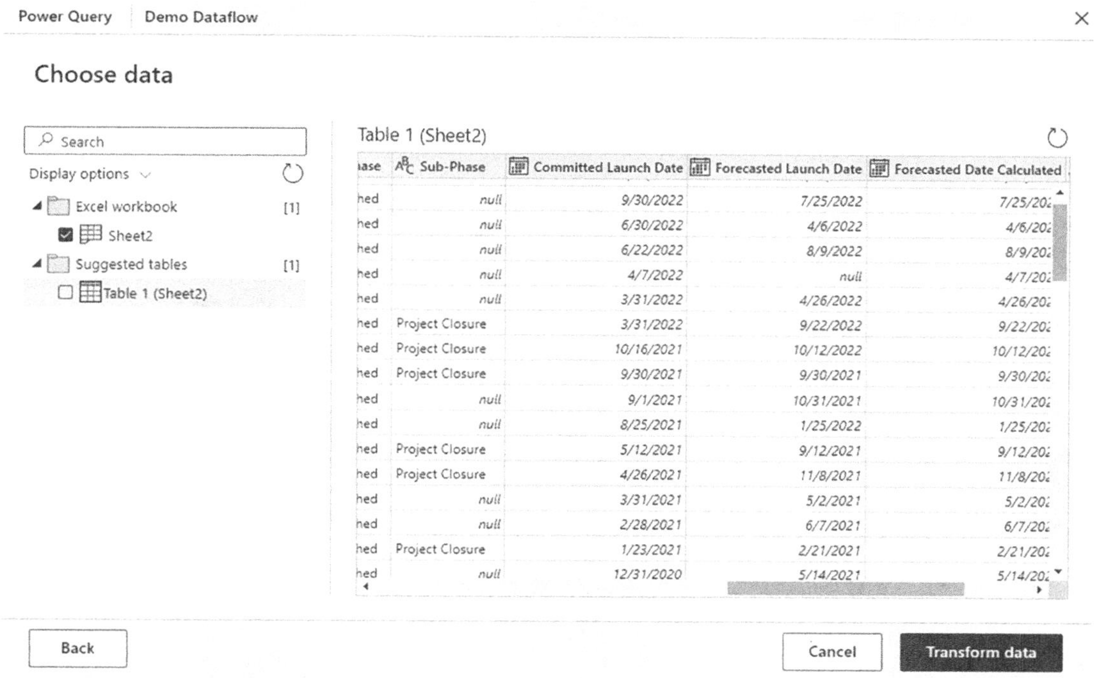

Figure 6-24. *Selecting sheets from Excel document*

A dialogue will open with Power Query where you can apply transformations to your data, such as filtering, grouping, formatting, and so on, as seen in Figure 6-25. As you manipulate the data, you will see that steps build on the right in Query Settings. This is helpful if you need to work backward to see what you did if your data is not looking right.

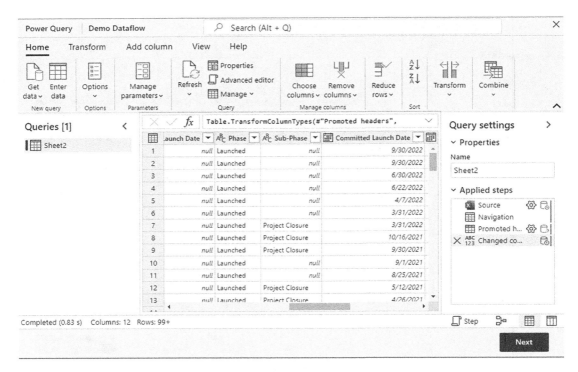

Figure 6-25. *Power Query designer*

Clicking Next brings you to the Map Tables dialogue, where you can define the properties of the tables you are moving the data into, as seen in Figure 6-26.

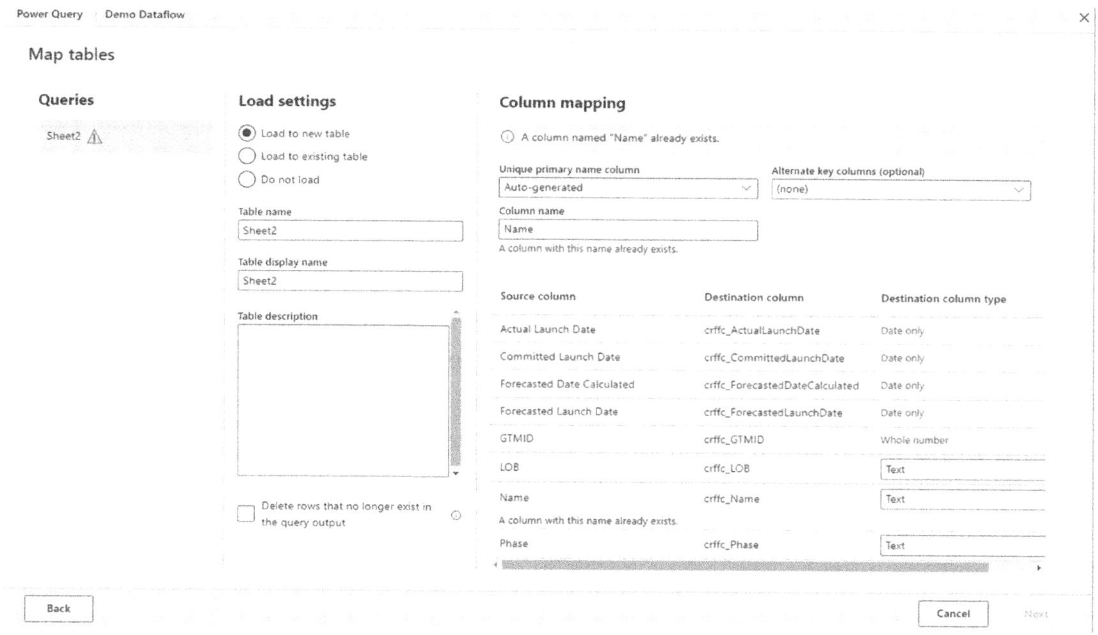

Figure 6-26. *Map Tables dialogue*

In the Load Settings section, specify whether you want to load to a new table or an existing one. There is also an option for Do Not Load, which is only if you want to use this dataflow to feed into another one.

Note   Selecting "Delete rows that no longer exist in the query output" will remove any rows created in your table from your dataflow but will also have a negative performance impact, which can be a problem for large datasets.

Selecting "Load to New Table" or "Load to Existing Table" will display the column mapping section where you will select the source column and destination column. Power Apps will attempt to set these by detecting column types, but any that are missing must be set.

Clicking Next brings you to the Refresh Settings screen, which allows you to configure the refresh to be either manual or automat based on a schedule.

Click Publish when you are done, and it will be active. Once the dataflow runs, you will have a table in Dataverse with the specified data ready to use.

Note   Dataflows cannot be created inside a solution but can be added afterward by selecting "Add Existing" and selecting the dataflow.

Summary

In conclusion, there are many ways to integrate Dataverse with other systems. Whether you must import data related to a migration, sync data from a legacy system to relate to records in your tool, or connect directly to other tools to create tickets, there is a solution to meet your needs. Next, you will learn how to go about planning sessions with your users and stakeholders to gather requirements and reduce rework.

CHAPTER 7

Planning Your Solution Design

One of the benefits of Power Platform is that the solution development process can be more iterative than with other platforms. However, you still want to approach your solution development with a plan in place to avoid the swirl of requirements that often happens with low-code/no-code platforms. This is even more important when you consider the data structure, security, and other underlying components of the backend of the solution. While apps and flows can easily be changed on the fly as requirements evolve or business needs change, if you do not have a solid foundation to your solution, it can become unstable, unpredictable, and unscalable.

In this chapter, we will discuss how to gather requirements, organize them in a meaningful way, communicate them to the business, test their assumptions, and develop iteratively to stay ahead of changes. It is not enough to simply listen to requirements and build to the specifications; you must challenge assumptions and poor design choices. You are the technology expert in the room, and, as such, your opinion matters. Saying "I told you so" is never as good as "I am happy everything is as expected."

Organizing Thoughts

One of the benefits of developing in a low-code/no-code environment is that you typically end up working closely with the business teams, which means you can be more involved in the requirements-gathering process. However, gathering requirements can be a challenging ordeal if you are unprepared for such an endeavor, especially since business users rarely understand concepts of data architecture.

© Brian Hodel 2023
B. Hodel, *Beginning Microsoft Dataverse*, https://doi.org/10.1007/978-1-4842-9334-8_7

Compare to Current

Often, there is an existing process or system that the business is operating in that they are trying to replace or improve. This can be a good opportunity to learn what they are trying to get out of the new solution. I will often set up time to just watch a user interact with the current tools and take notes of what they do along the way. This can help uncover opportunities to improve the process. Next, I will have the users tell me what they are doing as they do the work and describe what frustrates them about the process. Usually, what users find frustrating are the things that get in the way of getting work done, which is a good indicator that there may be waste in the process.

In lean manufacturing, waste is defined as anything that does not add value to a process; i.e., something that the customer is not willing to pay for. There are many definitions of the types of waste, but I am partial to the Toyota Production System's set, which uses TIMWOODS as a pneumonic device to remember them by. Those wastes are as follows:

- **Transportation**: Moving items or information when it is unnecessary. This can be seen in processes where data is copied from one place to another, or data is extracted and imported to another system. When possible, keeping a "single source of truth" is ideal.

- **Inventory**: Keeping more items or information than needed. It is common to store every document and record that is generated, when usually a summary or "lessons learned" can suffice instead.

- **Motion**: Excessive movement or travel. This can be things like traveling to a printer, scanner, fax, or file cabinet.

- **Waiting**: Waiting for information to arrive or action to be taken. This is commonly seen where steps require review or approval before moving to the next step.

- **Overprocessing**: Doing more work than is required. It is common for people to review and re-review records and documents for mistakes, even when mistakes are infrequent.

- **Overproduction**: Doing work before it is required. While people often look at "getting a jump on things" as a good thing, it often leads to rework as things upstream in the process change.

- **Defects**: Errors that need to be corrected. This is common when systems do not have data validation and review stages in place to prevent errors downstream.

- **Skills**: Employees working below their skill level. Not only is this a waste of resources, but it can also lead to dissatisfied employees because they are not challenged.

Having business users tell you what works and what does not work helps you to understand their needs and desires in a new tool. While most users will not readily identify wastes in a process, they will be happy to see those annoyances and barriers to getting work done disappear.

Keep a Steady Course

The 80/20 rule states that 80 percent of your work will be spent on 20 percent of the value. I have found this is often closer to 90/10, but the point persists. This is not only true of development, but also of requirements discussions. It is common for a room full of business users to spiral out of control about the edge cases in a process and how they are going to handle them. Not only is this time misdirected, but it also distracts from the core functionality and often causes significant issues to be overlooked.

To keep users on track and ensure their time is valuable, I attempt to steer the conversation in a more productive direction by encouraging them to question why the edge case exists and if it should at all. The "5 Whys" is an extremely easy and effective tool to find the root cause of an issue. Once a root cause is determined, it is often easier to determine that the edge case is the cause of some other issue that needs to be addressed instead of causing more work downstream.

The principal of the "5 Whys" is simple: ask "why" five times. By the fifth "why," you have a good idea what the issue is about. Here is an example:

- **Problem**: We need to accommodate expedited project plans for projects submitted within 90 days of launch.

- **Question**: Why do we need to accommodate expedited projects?

- **Answer**: Users enter projects too close to the launch date and the normal process does not allow for the speed required.

- **Q**: Why do users submit the projects so late?

- **A**: Because the review phases take a long time to get approved.

- **Q**: Why does it take so long to approve a phase?

- **A**: Because it requires a lot of time to launch the program, find the project, review the valuable information, and approve the phase.

- **Q**: Why are there so many steps to approve?

- **A**: Because the emails do not contain enough critical information or deep links to the project.

- **Q**: Why?

- **A**: Because we never added that functionality to the emails.

So, as you can see, once the team interrogated the issue more, it changed from needing to accommodate expedited projects, which causes a lot of chaos and added cost, to simply needing an easier way for approver to review and approve phases. By asking the users for more specifics on their reasoning, they found a root cause of the problem. Once you have a root cause, it is much easier to develop a solution and address the problem instead of accommodating variation in the process.

What I Am Hearing Is...

Getting users to question their assumptions is a frequent problem in requirements-gathering sessions because most people do not like to be wrong. Therefore, it is essential to develop tactics to make people feel like you are listening to them and respect their opinion, while also encouraging them to evolve their opinions when necessary.

One method of achieving this is active listening. Active listening is a process that encourages people to feel that you are listening to and comprehending their words, which in turn will break down some of their defensiveness. Here are some of the key pieces of active listening:

- **Non-Verbal Communication**: Maintaining eye contact, nodding your head, and avoiding defensive postures like crossing your arms are all important to showing you are receptive and attentive.

- **Paraphrasing or Reflecting**: Making statements such as "What I am hearing is . . ." or "Help me to understand . . ." shows you are listening but can also encourage them to see their point of view from a different angle.

- **Be Patient**: When someone stops talking, avoid the urge to start talking right away. Leaving a five- to ten-second pause does not sound like a lot but can be uncomfortable, encouraging people to keep talking to fill the space. Through this, they often rephrase and reevaluate their ideas.

- **Empathize**: People complaining about tools and processes can give good insight into trouble spots. A simple "That sounds annoying, can you tell me more about it?" can help discover opportunities for improvement.

Stay on the Path

While it is important to be receptive to innovative ideas and encourage the challenging of the status quo, it is equally important to manage expectations. I often say that anything is possible, but it is not all practical. Users produce a lot of great ideas, but it is your job as the developer to inform them of the cost of those ideas. It may be nice to have a convertible top on a car, but if you live in a wet climate, you may eventually wish someone had pointed out that they are not ideal for areas where it rains often. If users are informed up front that their feature may result in additional time, complexity, or instability, they may reconsider the feature or find another way to meet the need. It is also not bad to take the position that certain features will result in bad architecture and simply advise against it.

Sadly, you will not always win these arguments. There will be times when the business has a hard requirement regardless of complexity of implementation. The reality is that having "too many cooks in the kitchen" will cause issues. However, even the largest kitchens can run effectively if there is structure, order, and respect. Even though the process of working directly with the business can add complexity to the process, the benefits far outweigh the costs. Building a tool around the work instead of working around a tool will always end up with a better solution.

Developing Your Structures

Developing data and security structures is complex work that requires a lot of planning and technical understanding that business users really are not interested in. That said, the business users are the ones who will provide a great deal of the requirements that will inform the structures, so they need to be a part of the process of planning at some level.

I have found that the best way to engage business users in this process is to use basic diagrams and build it out with them while discussing the levels and relationships. Letting the business users lead you through the discussion, while you take notes and update the model, will help them think through how the data works together. This can be done in Visio, on a whiteboard, or even on sticky notes. The key is to keep it high level and stay out of the weeds.

Tip   While detailed diagrams and documentation can be overwhelming for some end users, try to use as much detail as you can to toe the line with them. Tools like Unified Modeling Language (UML) diagrams give you a very structured and powerful way to document requirements. Even if you don't use them with end users in workshops, it is a good tool to keep track of requirements as you go along.

Mapping the Data

It is difficult for business users to understand how they want to structure their data, especially when it comes to edge cases. Many times, users will outline a structure from a logical standpoint, but, once they try to apply data to it, it falls apart. To mitigate that, I build a basic structure and simply have them fill out the names of the records at each layer, as seen in Figure 7-1. By doing this, the users can see where there are gaps, or where they need additional layers or relationships. This is clearly not a technical diagram, but it helps non-technical people to work through the thought process.

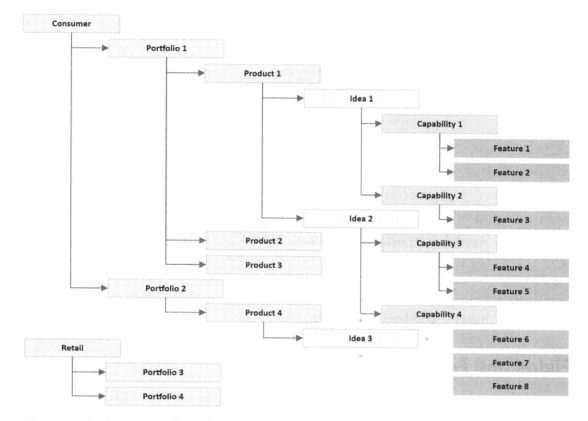

Figure 7-1. *Mapping data for business users*

Once we have figured out the data structures, we can discuss security layers by adding onto the existing model that we just built. You can take the model that we just built and add person and team icons, color coding them with the associated levels, to easily illustrate record permissions and inheritance, as seen in Figure 7-2.

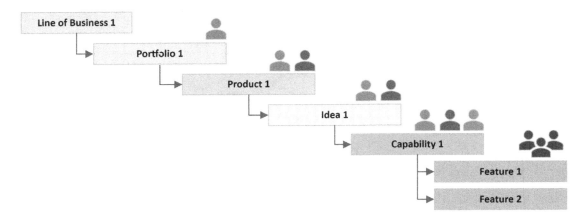

Figure 7-2. *Applying security roles to data model*

This sort of visual model makes it easy for a business user to think through the permissions structure in real scenarios and allows me, as a developer, to get the information that I need to begin designing.

Fields and Forms

Another challenge with requirements gathering is understanding the fields that need to be created for each table. While Dataverse does allow some flexibility in changing field types and properties, there are limits that will cause issues downstream, such as changing a single select to a multi-select field. Getting the field requirements up front will save a lot of rework in the process and frustration with both developers and business users.

One way to gather requirements is to create a spreadsheet with the field properties and share it with users to work on together, as seen in Figure 7-3.

Form Section	Field Name	Field Type	Required	Conditional
Project Info	Autodesk Account Hub	Text	TRUE	FALSE
Project Info	Client Name	Text	TRUE	FALSE
Project Info	Street	Text	TRUE	FALSE
Project Info	City	Auto	TRUE	FALSE
Project Info	State Province	Auto	TRUE	FALSE
Project Info	Zip Code	Auto	TRUE	FALSE
Project Info	Country	Auto	TRUE	FALSE
Project Info	Start Date	Date	TRUE	FALSE
Project Info	End Date	Date	TRUE	FALSE
Project Info	Time Zone	Dropdown	TRUE	FALSE
Project Info	Region	Dropdown	TRUE	FALSE
Planning & Turnover	Scope	Combobox	TRUE	FALSE
Planning & Turnover	Design Deliverables	Combobox	TRUE	FALSE
Planning & Turnover	Schedule Exists	Y/N	TRUE	FALSE
Planning & Turnover	Client File Exchange Reqs	Y/N	TRUE	FALSE
Planning & Turnover	Client BIM/CAD Reqs	Y/N	TRUE	FALSE
Planning & Turnover	Collab Platform Host	Dropdown	TRUE	FALSE
Planning & Turnover	Design Authoring Platforms	Combobox	TRUE	FALSE
Planning & Turnover	Data Secuity Reqs	Y/N	TRUE	FALSE
Planning & Turnover	Digital Signatures Allowed	Y/N	TRUE	FALSE
Planning & Turnover	Existing Condition Files	Combobox	TRUE	FALSE
Planning & Turnover	Record Component Reqd	Y/N	TRUE	FALSE

Figure 7-3. *Field requirements-gathering spreadsheet*

This technique can save you, as a developer, time by not having to gather the requirements yourself and allowing users to think through the requirements that make up the fields. Using Excel Online makes this process much more friendly as you can track all changes, leave notes, and assign tasks to users by tagging them in the comments. This collaborative process can save time and reduce confusion.

Some of the key attributes that you want to gather are as follows:

- **Form Section**: Whether or not the forms are separated into sections, it often helps to organize the fields into groups to establish logical relationships between the data.

- **Field Name**: Capturing the display name of the field is necessary. Gathering the technical name is optional.

- **Field Type**: Type of field. It is not necessary to specify the detailed field types, but focus on being specific enough to avoid having to recreate fields later.

- **Required**: Specify if the field is required or not.

- **Conditional**: Specify if the field has conditional requirements on it.

- **Conditions**: Define the conditions applied to the field, such as when it is visible, required, or options are filtered.

- **Guidance Text**: Hover text, placeholder text, and subtext are all common types of guidance text related to fields.

- **Field Security**: Specify any security requirements around the field.

- **Comments**: It never hurts to have some open text space for users to make notes or leave additional instructions.

Although the fields are created on the tables, it can be easier for business users to think of things as forms instead of tables. This also allows you more freedom to architect the data in a way that works best for the solution. Encourage users to focus on the process and what needs to be tracked instead of how it is accomplished so they do not get lost in the details.

Don't Skimp on the Details

As you work through the process of requirements gathering, you will begin filling in gaps. Just like if you were to start with a jar full of rocks, then add pebbles, then sand, your requirements will continue to develop as a solid mass and become more solid. As this happens, be aware that cracks may start to form in the logic of the build. Record structures may not align with the permissions requirements, a fixed number of values may need to change to a scalable collection of values, or an approval process may need to be able to accommodate groups instead of just users. These are things that you will want to watch for and bring up to the users as you continue to gather requirements. It is very much a back-and-forth discussion of what the needs are and what is practical to build.

One method of managing requirements, especially at this level, is to compile a list of the requirements and rate them so they can be organized by priority. A simple method is to simply assign them each as Must Have, Should Have, Nice to Have, and Backlog.

I usually add the backlog option so users have a place to put things that are not that important anymore, but that they do not want to lose sight of. Reassuring users that their time and efforts are valuable goes a long way to ensuring the process moves forward without hiccups.

Walking the Process

Workflows can be a daunting task to get requirements for. There are so many decisions and operations, as well as error handling and optimizations, that it can be overwhelming for business users who "just want it to work." The most successful sessions I led involved people from various roles who may interact with the proposed processes. The diverse perspectives add a lot of value to the discussions and break the core team out of their assumptions. I also find it valuable to be a bit hands-off for these, acting more as a moderator than a contributor. This allows the team to think through the processes and take ownership of them. This does not work for all teams, but there is a lot of value when you can utilize it.

Preparing for Workshop

The first step is to map the process. If you already have a process, this can be a bit faster because you will start by mapping the current process. If you do not have one yet, then start by mapping the process as it should be.

I prefer to do this by hosting an in-person workshop so the team can have time to really think through problems and discuss how things work or should work. It is amazing how, even in the most rigorously controlled environments, different people will have drastically different opinions on how the process works, and it is almost never what is documented.

Note   While I have found that in-person workshops are the most effective, using tools like Microsoft Teams with chat and whiteboards can be very effective and accommodate teams where in-person is difficult to accommodate. Hybrid workshops can also be effective if you can ensure that the remote team members are not neglected.

Before the session, collect a variety of sticky notes in assorted colors, markers, poster paper, and painter's tape. Set up a poster paper as a key or legend with one of each sticky note and describe what that color means, such as start, end, approval, decision, and so on. It is also a good idea to have smaller keys printed out that can be posted at each section of the room so the teams can easily refer to them. Next, attach poster paper to the walls around the room. The poster paper is where the team will map the processes and allows you to remove the processes to keep for later sessions. If you have a room where you can leave them up throughout the entire process, that is ideal.

Note   You should test your sticky notes on the walls or poster paper before your session to ensure they stick. Some sticky notes do not play well with certain surfaces, and you do not want a workshop where the notes keep falling off the walls!

Mapping the Current State

During the workshop, introduce everyone to process mapping by mapping out a sample process, like sending an email, just to get them used to the types of steps and how to think in the process mindset of start and end. Next, break the team into smaller groups and assign them processes to work on. Your role is to facilitate the session, help with questions and disputes, and ask leading questions about the process that helps the teams think through problems. If you have advanced processes, you may need to talk about how swim-lane process maps work and how to set them up. A swim-lane process map organizes the process steps in a series of lanes that indicate which team the step belongs to, as seen in Figure 7-4.

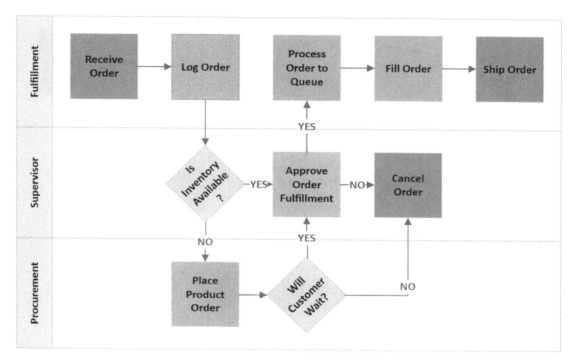

Figure 7-4. *Process mapping with sticky notes*

In the end, you will have a bunch of process maps like those seen in Figure 7-4.

Note   The Post-it corporation has a great app for capturing Post-it notes from a wall and saving them in the app for future reference. It is a clever way to document your process maps if you want to preserve them or use them later.

Interrogate the Process

The next part of the workshop, or a separate workshop, is centered around identifying waste in the process. You will need to discuss the concepts of what waste is and how to identify it, but it is a fun and valuable exercise where the team can take stickers or smaller sticky notes and put them wherever they see waste. You can even find some caution or warning stickers for this step to break the mood a bit. It is never a bad thing to have fun while working!

When you are done with this session, you will have a bunch of marks on your processes where the team has identified waste, as seen in Figure 7-5.

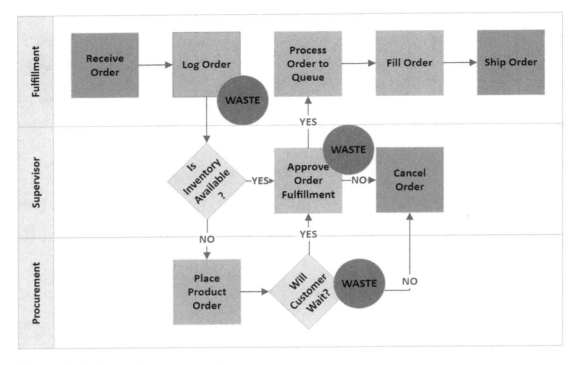

Figure 7-5. *Identifying waste in process map*

If you want to get fancy, you can identify the types of waste and quantify them, but that is not necessary for building a tool unless you want to quantify the business impact of the changes.

Improve the Process

After you have identified the waste in the processes, you can begin finding solutions to those problems. This part of the process can be a lot of fun, but also cause a lot of conflict, so there are some things to keep track of.

When in Doubt, Throw It Out

Teams often assume that things are done for a reason and cannot be changed. It is surprising how often a process can have unnecessary steps because no one ever really pushed back on whether it was necessary. This process can be uncomfortable at first, but usually gathers momentum as teams see how liberating it is. To encourage users to challenge the current process, it helps to have an outlined evaluation process set up, like the one seen in Figure 7-6.

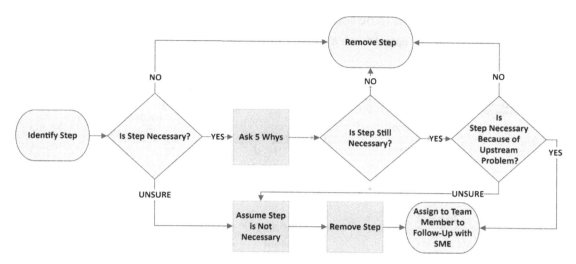

Figure 7-6. *Step evaluation process*

By having an established evaluation process, users are more likely to challenge the norms because they don't have to own the decisions themselves and they can feel confident that assumptions will be evaluated with the correct people.

Assume, but Do Not Forget

There will inevitably be questions that cannot be answered in the workshop. Instead of stopping with the process, simply make an assumption, document it, and move on with that assumption. At the end of the session, assign people to verify the assumptions with the appropriate teams. Again, having a process and a template for documenting assumptions, as well as any other important data points, not only keeps things organized, but also puts the users at ease because they know there is a level of accountability and control in place to balance the uncertainty of challenging the familiar. This also helps to reinforce the fact that good processes can be a help instead of a hindrance.

Find the Root Cause

It is not always easy to find the root cause of a problem, and teams will often add more waste to a process in trying to solve a problem; for example, adding more inspection points to a process instead of adding data validation upstream to prevent errors. Encourage the teams to use root-cause analysis tools to ensure the problem being solved is indeed the one that needs to be solved. The "5 Whys" is a great tool, but there are many other tools that are easy to use and very effective, such as the fishbone diagram seen in Figure 7-7.

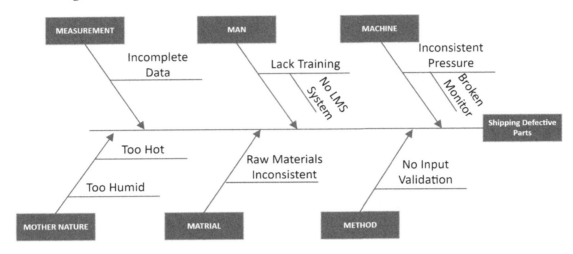

Figure 7-7. *Fishbone diagram example*

The fishbone diagram is great for larger root-cause analysis work where a defect may have multiple contributing factors. Start by listing the defect at the head of the "fish," then set up the primary branches with the primary causes of the defect. The "6Ms" listed in Figure 7-7 are standard but feel free to adjust them as needed. From there, work your way down each "bone," identifying causes, then contributing causes. The more granular you get, the more root causes you can identify. This also works well with the "5 Whys" because as you ask the Whys, you will uncover various root causes, and this can be a way to document those.

Since you may have a tough time working on all the items at once, using a system of voting by the team might help to narrow down the top contributors to the problem. By giving every team member a set number of sticks, say two each, they can place them on the cause that they feel has the highest impact on the defect. Ideally, this would be done in an analytical method using data, but voting can get you going in a good direction during workshops or when data is lacking.

Build with the End in Mind

An often-overlooked aspect of solution design is that practically every tool will need to have reporting capabilities. While your data structures will obviously provide data that can be reported on, it is easy to run into situations where the granularity of data that is desired for reporting is not captured in the system, or it is overly complex to extract it from the structures that were developed to enable functionality. By including reporting and analytics as part of your requirements-gathering process, even if the scope of work does not include it, you can ensure that you are prepared for it when it comes along.

Summary

In summary, the best solutions are built when the solution design and requirements gathering are done in parallel in an iterative approach. This process relies not only on clear documentation, but also on effective communication and expectation management. Realizing the business users are not technical and meeting them at a level that they are comfortable with will make for a productive engagement and a better solution build.

Index

A

© Brian Hodel 2023
B. Hodel, *Beginning Microsoft Dataverse*, https://doi.org/10.1007/978-1-4842-9334-8

D

Printed in the United States
by Baker & Taylor Publisher Services